FINDING
Your Way to
HAPPY

25 Invaluable Lessons for Life

BRAD ANASTASIA

RESERVE HOUSE
PUBLISHING

Chicago

Reserve House books are available at special discounts when publishing in bulk.
Special editions or book excerpts also can be created to specification. For details or
media enquiries, contact the Special Sales Director at the address, phone, or email below.

RESERVE HOUSE
PUBLISHING

Reserve House Publishing
P.O. Box 101061
Chicago, IL 60610-1061
(312) 725-0795
reservehouse@gmail.com

Library of Congress Cataloging-in-Publication Data
Anastasia, Brad.
Finding your way to happy: twenty-five invaluable lessons for life / by Brad Anastasia.
p. cm.
ISBN 978-0-615-57752-4
2012901387

Cover design by Alan Pranke
Interior design by Sunny B. DiMartino

Printed in the United States of America

For My Mom

The love you showed me was the greatest lesson a son could ever learn.
I miss you so much.

"From the beginning to the end, life is a school, complete with individualized tests and challenges. When we've learned all we can possibly learn, and when we have taught all we can possibly teach, we return home."

—Elizabeth Kübler-Ross & David Kessler, *Life Lessons*

CONTENTS

NOTE TO READERS

The lessons in this book appear in no particular order, and each is self-contained, so feel free to skip around as you wish. This book is a guide not a novel, so you'll likely get the most out of it by reading a chapter or two at a time and then contemplating what you've learned before continuing on.

INTRODUCTION

I don't have a Ph.D., I'm not an expert in any field of psychology, and, most notably, I'm only thirty-five years old. Given those facts, what gave me the absurd idea that I was qualified to write a book about essential life lessons? More importantly, why should you bother to read it? It's true that I don't have the requisite experience to be considered an authority in any field of human behavior, much less a writer. However, everyone has a talent they consider to be their greatest strength, and for me that talent is an instinctive understanding of how to live a good life.

So much of what goes into living a good life lies in figuring out what you need (and don't need) to be happy, as well as avoiding the common mistakes most people make throughout life. There are generally two ways to acquire this knowledge: learning from your own personal experiences (trial and error) and learning from those who have already traversed a similar path to the one you're on now. Although both can be valuable, learning from the latter gives you a head start on life's timeless lessons, and helps you avoid saying those dreaded words: *If I only knew then what I know now.* That is the reason why I wrote this book, and why I think you should read it.

WHAT THEY SHOULD HAVE TAUGHT YOU IN SCHOOL

I've always thought how great it would be if every school had a class called Life 101. In this hypothetical class, you'd get educated in the type of knowledge that helps you live a happy, meaningful life. For instance, the curriculum might include how to find a career you're passionate about, what qualities you should look for in a compatible life partner, what leads to good health and longevity, how to manage your finances prudently, and what to expect in life as you grow older. Sadly, the social institutions that could be providing this invaluable knowledge—our schools, government, and religious organizations—usually have a different agenda that they need to adhere to, and that agenda is not always congruent with our personal best interests. Even friends and family, well-intentioned as they are, cannot always be relied upon to help us navigate the myriad of obstacles, pitfalls, and dilemmas that we're bound to face throughout life. In the absence of all that, I hope this book helps fill in some of the gaps.

Now, I'm certainly not naive enough to believe you can learn everything about life from books, classes, or other secondhand knowledge. Despite the counsel of others who claim to know best (including your humble author), you still need to go out into the world and learn certain things on your own, and in your own way. With that in mind, this book is not intended to replace real-life experience, but instead to serve as a useful guide that helps you make smart, informed decisions whenever these lessons materialize in your life.

ON FINDING YOUR WAY TO HAPPY

One of the rules I established with myself while writing this book was that everything must be completely honest, so I will speak openly about my own life experiences, including mistakes I've made that I'm not proud of, insecurities I've been plagued by, and other issues I continue to struggle with and need to work on. I also wanted to ensure that anything I wrote was totally in sync with what I believe. The best way to teach is to lead by example, and I wasn't about to provide advice to anyone if I wasn't one-hundred-percent willing to adhere to that same advice myself.

I'm also not going to make any unsubstantiated promises about how this book will help you change into a different person overnight, be happy forever, or lose ten pounds. Reading this book, or any self-help book for that matter, is just one step in a long, multi-faceted process toward self-improvement, where the burden of responsibility falls on you. Making lasting improvements in your life requires not only an understanding of what to do, but constant reminders, real-world practice, and plenty of patience as well.

Lastly, it's fair to say that this book deals a lot with learning how to avoid the common pitfalls of life. But it's also about learning to recognize opportunities for growth and happiness whenever they present themselves, and not hesitating to go after them when they do. Understanding how to do *both* is fundamentally important to living a good life. Playing your only hand in life too conservatively may spare you a good deal of pain and suffering, but it also denies you some of life's greatest pleasures and rewards that result from being spontaneous, taking good risks, and stepping outside of your comfort zone.

"Happiness is not simply the absence of despair. It is an affirmative state in which our lives have both meaning and pleasure."

—Gordon Livingston, *Too Soon Old, Too Late Smart*

FINDING
Your Way to
HAPPY

FORGET THE RAT RACE—
TRY THE OTHER DIRECTION

*"Now, here, you see, it takes all the running you can do,
to keep in the same place. If you want to get somewhere else,
you must run at least twice as fast as that!"*

—Lewis Carroll, *Through the Looking-Glass*

In today's competitive society, everyone is looking to get ahead. Whether it's working hard to earn more money or to secure a fancy new title, the belief is that contentment is just one bonus or promotion away. It doesn't matter if you hate your job or are stressed out beyond belief, as long as you "get there." But here's the rub. No matter how hard you try, you will never get there, because there will always be more money to make, more expensive things to buy, and more important positions to work toward. What you once thought was a fair race actually turns out to be a treadmill where, despite all of the effort you put in, you're still in the same place where you started (and none the more content). The unfortunate truth is: you're trying to compete in an un-winnable race.

IT'S WHAT YOU CAN HANDLE, NOT WHAT YOU HAVE

What many people don't realize is that the true path to contentment actually lies in the opposite direction. In other words, instead of constantly struggling to have more and get ahead, we should be focusing our efforts on learning how to be content with less. Although this may sound counterintuitive based on our society's definition of success, you'll be amazed at how much your life can improve by making this critical adjustment.

As I am writing this, the global economy is still reeling from a significant recession, the likes of which most of us have never experienced. As much as I sympathize with the people who have suffered as a result of this economic downturn, I know that in the end it will provide some useful lessons. The news is full of stories about people who have lost their jobs, their home, or both, and have to cope with a new reality that was not of their choosing. The irony is that, instead of the world coming to an end as many feared, most are discovering that they can actually live with a lot less and still be happy. In fact, most of the material things we believe we "have to have" are easily discarded without another thought when the rent needs to be paid or the kids need to be fed.

What many people are now realizing is that they are much better at handling things than they gave themselves credit for, and that accumulating money and material possessions only offers a false sense of security. Although these things can be useful to an extent, it's what you can handle, not what you have, that offers greater peace of mind. My hope is that these important realizations will not be forgotten once things turn around again (which they always do).

VOLUNTARILY EXIT

I spent over five years working as an investment banker in New York City, which is the epitome of the rat race. I was always so concerned with making money and getting ahead, but sadly I never analyzed what I needed that much money for, or whether it was actually making me any happier. The more I lived that lifestyle, the more it seemed I needed, creating an endless cycle of working to consume. I wish I could say that I at least felt happier with my newfound wealth and possessions, but it was just the opposite. I was stressed out beyond belief, my hair started to fall out, and I became quite depressed.

After spending many somber nights analyzing the situation at my local Starbucks, I finally figured out where I went wrong. All this time I had been operating under the very false premise that more money correlates with more happiness, and I was finally beginning to see the error of my ways. One thing was certain: the path I was currently on would not lead to the contentment I was seeking. There had to be a better way, and I was determined to find it.

The first thing I knew that needed to be done was to quit my high-paying, unbelievably stressful job, and get the hell out of the rat race before I did any further damage to my well-being. I clearly remember thinking that even if my company tried to entice me to stay by doubling my salary, I would refuse. I mean, how could I put a dollar value on my health and happiness? Still, it was a decision that came with a great deal of fear and required a huge leap of faith that I was doing the right thing.

Once I worked up the courage to leave my job, I figured it was time to get a new perspective on things. So I packed up a suitcase, ditched my apartment, and boarded a plane to South America in search of a simpler life. It was a good move, because my experience there would forever change my view of what is needed in life to be truly content.

During my travels, I spent numerous days and nights on crowded buses and in small hostels that offered only the most basic necessities. At first I resisted this lifestyle adjustment, because I was so accustomed to living in New York with all of its conveniences and luxuries. But what I quickly realized is that living this way had no lasting negative effect on my mood or outlook. I had a stack of books, my iPod, good food, a hot shower, and a warm bed. Occasionally, friends from back home would visit and I'd even have a traveling companion as well. All of this was more than enough to make me feel content. Would I have preferred a first-class plane ride or a five-star hotel with all of its comforts? Of course, but my point is that those luxuries didn't offer anything that would make a lasting difference to my well-being, so there was no need to struggle to obtain them as I had been doing in my former life.

What ultimately destroyed any remaining doubt I had that the rat race was a fool's game was the many local people I encountered throughout my travels. Most of these people existed on so little, yet they were so welcoming, positive, and generous with the little that they did have. I had to chuckle at the irony of comparing them to those who had so much (myself included), yet were miserable and always struggling to get more. All of those experiences helped reinforce the idea that it's not necessary to "have it all," because happiness and contentment can come from having so much less than we think.

DON'T BE ENSLAVED
BY WHAT YOU DON'T NEED

So how do you voluntarily exit the rat race and get on the *real* path to contentment? It begins with taking a very honest look at how you're making your money and what you're spending it on. For example, are you working hard at a job you dislike just so you can save up for a bigger, more expensive home? It seems many people are in this same predicament, struggling to burden themselves with a huge mortgage that, ironically, will necessitate working even harder to maintain.

How much additional stress goes into that extra work? Is anything getting sacrificed irreparably in the process such as your health, time with family, or time to yourself? When those real costs are added to the equation, all that effort doesn't seem to add any net positive benefit to well-being, especially in light of how little effect material goods have on long-term happiness. Working at a job you dislike to buy a bigger house is just an example, but struggling to accumulate anything that has no long-term contribution to happiness is equally futile. In fact, taking the time to really analyze what you spend your hard-earned money on, versus what actually makes you happy, can lead to some very interesting revelations about what you truly need in life (not to mention the amount of stress you could spare yourself).

One exercise that has helped me tremendously is to sit down and actually write out what my current *needs* are and how much they cost to fulfill. This list includes things like a monthly food budget, rent, insurance, good books, and trips home to visit my family—all of which I consider essential and form a significant component of my happiness. Unsurprisingly absent from the list are several "nice to haves" such as designer clothes, upscale living arrangements, and that SUV I've always wanted. By putting this list together, I quickly realized that I had a lot more freedom in my life than I had previously thought. More importantly, with my wealth expectations significantly lowered, I had greater flexibility to choose a career that was more congruent with my passions and desired lifestyle.

By taking a few minutes to do this exercise yourself, it will quickly become clear that the things you need to be happy are significantly easier to obtain (and a lot less expensive) than all of those things that you'd "like to have." Review your list often to see if there are other unnecessary expenses you can cut out, because with each new cut comes greater freedom from the rat race. Ultimately this new perspective will provide you with more flexibility in your choice of careers, and free up extra time that could be spent on things more meaningful to you. As opposed to a larger bank account or a bigger home, these benefits *will* lead to happier outcomes.

"We are enriched not by what we possess, but by what we can do without."

—Immanuel Kant

THE RAT RACE IS ONLY PAINFUL IF YOU CHOOSE TO STAY IN IT

Don't get me wrong. Exiting the rat race voluntarily is not something easily done. It takes a big leap of faith to trust that you don't need as much as you think, as well as a strong sense of self-worth to tune out those who falsely believe that accumulated wealth is the ultimate judge of a person's success in life. Capitalistic society has evolved to the point where not competing in the rat race can lead to feelings of insecurity and fear that you are not doing enough to remain competitive with the imaginary status quo.

But when you think about it, what exactly are you concerned might happen if you decide to leave the rat race on your own terms? Are you afraid your wife will leave you for someone richer, your kids won't go to private school, or the Joneses will secretly scoff at your less than 3,000-square-foot home? Are these fears even legitimate, and if so, whatever gave you the idea that struggling to avoid these outcomes would make you happier anyway?

What we really should fear is spending our time and energy laboring under the false assumption that the more we accumulate the closer we are to contentment. If you need more evidence to convince you of this, have a look around you. Do you really see a direct correlation between happiness and accumulated wealth? I don't. In fact I used to be one of those "successful" guys always struggling to have more, and believe me, I was not any happier for it. Actually, I was completely miserable. So before you struggle another day in your life to reach contentment by having it all, please heed this advice and trust that the real path to contentment lies in the other direction. I leave you with the wise words of Nassim Taleb, who sums this sentiment up best:

> "Missing a train is only painful if you run after it! Likewise, not matching the idea of success others expect from you is only painful if that's what you are seeking. You stand above the rat race and the pecking order, not outside of it, if you do so by choice. Quitting a high-paying position, if it is your decision, will seem a better payoff than the utility of the money involved (this may seem crazy, but I've tried it and it works)." [1]

---

1 Nassim Nicholas Taleb, *The Black Swan*

——————————— LESSON ———————————

True contentment will not be found by winning the rat race. No one wins that race, and you'll only wind up running in place, despite the money, things, or titles you accumulate. Although it may sound counterintuitive based on society's perception of success, true contentment can only be found in the opposite direction, by learning to live with less.

BE CONGRUENT

"Your life changes the moment you make a new, congruent, and committed decision."

—Anthony Robbins, *Awaken the Giant Within*

You don't have to be cool, rich, or attractive to obtain success in life. A much more relevant determinant is how *congruent* you are. In order to become more congruent, strive to meet the following three conditions:

- Comfortable in your own skin
- Beliefs, words, and actions in harmony
- Purpose in everything you do

When you are able to achieve this level of congruence, the world is yours for the taking.

COMFORTABLE IN YOUR OWN SKIN

People who are comfortable in their own skin are easy to spot. They are noticeably at ease in voice, body language, and appearance at all times, and don't feel the need to go out of their way to impress anybody. Essentially what they are sub-communicating is: *what you see is what you get*. When someone is unafraid to be real about who they are, imperfections and all, we are drawn to them because we know we aren't perfect either.

Contrast that to people who aren't comfortable in their own skin. They usually appear self-conscious, and always seem to be trying a little too hard to fit in. They are easy to spot as well, but for different reasons (a fake laugh, awkward body language, an ill-suited outfit). It's hard to blame people for acting this way because it's natural to want to be universally liked. However, that's a completely unrealistic expectation if you want to be your true self.

I don't care if you are the nicest, sweetest, most conforming person in the world; there will still be people who won't care for you for whatever particular reason. The sooner you can accept that, the sooner you can stop worrying about what others think, and get on with being comfortable being who you are.

BELIEFS, WORDS, AND ACTIONS IN HARMONY

Achieving the level of congruence where your beliefs, words, and actions are in harmony with each other is no simple task. Recent hypocritical acts by some of our so-called role models demonstrate this repeatedly. Whether it's athletes who advocate good sportsmanship while finding ways to cheat, or priests who claim to be "men of God" while committing atrocious acts, hypocritical people are found in all walks of life and incite a great deal of anger in those who once looked up to them.

So what does thinking, saying, and doing in harmony actually look like? Picture someone like Mahatma Gandhi. He had an interminable desire to do good in the world, and lived his life in a way that was fully congruent with that goal. His thoughts were constantly focused on how he might help others, and anyone who listened to him speak noticed the genuine passion in his voice for what he was trying to achieve. As history has documented, he acted on his congruent beliefs and words by using his strongest efforts to make the world a better place. Gandhi's life is a great example of what can be achieved if you are fully congruent in what you believe, say, and do. There was no magic secret. He was just a fully congruent person who had an amazing dedication to his life's work.

Even if leading a nation of a billion-plus people is not one of your life goals, reaching this level of congruence is something anyone can achieve and use to their advantage. Maybe you have more modest desires like becoming successful at your job, finding a life partner, or becoming a better person. It really doesn't matter what your objective is, as long as your desire is genuine. Once you can take that initial desire and assimilate it fully into your thoughts, words, and actions (essentially, your entire being), the sky is the limit.

PURPOSE IN EVERYTHING YOU DO

By "purpose," I mean anything done with the intention of contributing to your happiness or personal growth. Things done with a purpose are congruent with who you are, what you believe in, and what you'd like to attain in life. Before making any significant decisions, you should always ask yourself whether the action you plan on taking has a clear purpose. It doesn't matter if you are contemplating getting married or having kids, it's never a rhetorical question to ask. If the action you plan on taking isn't going to improve your well-being, or bring you closer to a life goal, then what's the *purpose* of doing it at all?

A real consequence of doing things without purpose is *opportunity cost*. Opportunity cost can be defined as: missing out on a potential life-improving opportunity as a result of being preoccupied with something else. Many of the choices we make with regard to relationships, jobs, and how we spend our free time, can result in an opportunity cost of some kind.

The best way to minimize these costs is to never settle for less than what you deserve, and to only do things that serve a real purpose. Finding a true love in your life is no exception. I used to tease my friends when they would go on dates with someone they knew they weren't that into. I would tell them, "The potential love of your life is waiting for you tonight at Starbucks, the movies, or a bar, and you're blowing it by going on a date with someone you're not even interested in!" It was obviously all in jest, but there was also a large degree of truth to what I was saying. The point is that you shouldn't spend even a second of your life carrying out purposeless acts that come with high opportunity costs.

EMBRACE YOURSELF, AND CONGRUENCE WILL FOLLOW

Reaching a higher level of congruence starts with taking an honest inventory of who you are, what you value, and what you'd like to attain in your life. If meeting your soul mate is an important life goal, don't spend your time in relationships that you know have no potential. If you want to have meaning in your work, don't accept a job that conflicts with your personal values. If you want to have genuine friendships, be genuine and allow others to love and respect you for who you are, not for some phony social façade. Remember: the goal is not to be universally liked or to meet someone else's definition of success. The goal is to be true to yourself.

A lot of times our unhappiness can be traced back to the fact that we aren't being true to ourselves in some way. Despite our outward behavior, we have a persistent little voice in the back of our heads that says, "This isn't who you are!" When I look back on my younger years, it's easy to pinpoint how incongruent I was. I spent so much of my time staying out late drinking, acting like a tough guy, dating girls I had no serious interest in, and working at meaningless jobs that I absolutely despised. These are all things I did against my true character in order to fit in or meet someone else's idea of success, and it made me miserable.

Now I know better. Now I can say with pride that I'm a morning person, I don't like to drink, I'm empathetic to others' feelings, and I want to make a positive difference in this world through meaningful work. It feels so good to acknowledge these things about myself and not to have to fake anything. In no way am I claiming that I've reached full congruence, because I haven't. Every day I discover something new about myself, and it's a constant learning curve. But with more congruence comes greater assurance that this is who I truly am, and that this is how I should be living my life.

LESSON

To be congruent means that everything you do in life serves a real purpose given who you are, what you value, and what you'd like to attain. More than anything, reaching a high level of congruence is achieved by being true to yourself, not by conforming to someone else's definition of success or likability.

LIVE IN THE NOW

"You can't argue with what is. Well, you can, but if you do, you suffer."
—Eckhart Tolle, *The Power of Now*

How most people feel in any given moment is largely determined by two things: past events that they can't change, and the anticipation of future events (good or bad) that may never be realized. Yet lost in between the two is something that could offer a much more stable source of enjoyment: the present moment. The present moment is the *only* time when real happiness can be experienced. So why do so many of us have trouble enjoying the present moment for what it is? The answer is that we spend too much of our time searching for happiness in time periods that we have no control over. Instead of focusing on the one thing that we can control (how we feel *right now)*, we dwell on a past that's already gone, or wait in vain for the promise of an uncertain future.

WHERE YOU WON'T FIND HAPPINESS: THE PAST

Dwelling on negative past events that can't be changed is one of the most futile ways a person can spend their time. The only useful purpose it serves is to learn from previous mistakes and experiences. That's all. Once the learning has been accomplished, rehashing unpleasant past events and feeling bad over them just gives them unneeded attention, and negatively affects an innocent bystander: the present.

Looking at parts of your past with rose-colored glasses can also have negative consequences in the present. For example, have you ever found yourself longing for the good old days when everything was *seemingly* so much better with that ex-lover of yours? What in reality may have been a difficult period for you, is now remembered as the time of your life. In fact, you may even question why you ever left that "perfect" person in the first place! Instead of acknowledging that you probably had very good reasons for moving on at the time, selective memory conveniently shades out the negative details you'd rather not recall (the annoying habits, the bitter arguments, etc.).

Past memories are like a running movie, which we can edit however we see fit. Of course, it all happens at the expense of the present. By just being what it is, real, the present seems less sexy, especially when compared with that new and improved version of the past that we can create in our head.

Another way to get stuck in the past is by relying on "woulda, coulda, shoulda." It's far too easy to devalue the present by contemplating hypo-thetical past actions that *might* have improved our current situation. Here are a few examples:

- I love my wife, but I *should have* waited longer to get married.

- If the weather was warmer, this vacation *would have* been better.

- If only I *could have* gotten that promotion, then I'd really be happy.

Even if you don't actually say these words out loud, just thinking about what would've, could've, or should've happened in your life can take away from an otherwise enjoyable present. More importantly, there's no way of knowing if the present would actually be better if those things had happened, so a person is much better served by accepting *what is* than by contemplating *what might have been.*

Thinking about positive past memories that make you feel good is an acceptable way to contemplate the past, as long as it doesn't blind you to new opportunities for enjoyment in the present. If you look for happiness to arrive in the same form as it did in the past because *that is how you remember it to be,* then you'll likely miss new opportunities for happiness in the here and now.

For the longest time I was held back by the memory of how I first met a past girlfriend. Everything happened perfectly the night we met, from the initial glance to the goodnight kiss, and it was without a doubt love at first sight. The memory of that night conjured up so many pleasant feelings that I would often think back on it.

The only problem was, after we broke up, I got it stuck in my head that those same conditions had to be present (perfect night, love at first sight) if I was ever going to meet someone special again. Anytime I met someone new, I would discount any chance of a potential relationship if things didn't start out perfectly, like they did in the memory I was clinging to. I was limiting myself by expecting the present to play out just like I remembered the past, instead of being open to new opportunities for happiness that I had yet to experience.

WHERE YOU WON'T FIND HAPPINESS EITHER: THE FUTURE

I'm a big believer in setting goals and having things to look forward to. Both of these activities require planning for the future, but make us feel good and motivate us in the present. However, in order not to devalue the present, it's crucial to do two things: manage your expectations and enjoy the ride.

It's fun planning for future events, such as a wedding, vacation, or night out on the town. The anticipation of those events conjures up pleasant images in our minds, and gives us something positive to look forward to. However, sometimes we can look forward to something so much, that anything we do up until then just seems like killing time before getting to the *real* enjoyment! Doing this not only detracts from the present, but makes it nearly impossible for that future event to meet our built-up expectations, ultimately leaving us disappointed. This is undoubtedly a lose/lose situation.

So how do you realistically convince yourself not to get overly excited about future events, lest you wind up let down? Unless you're a monk who has renounced all attachments, it's difficult, but not impossible. Instead of depending on some future event to be the savior that improves your well-being, focus more on making the present as enjoyable as possible.

Take retirement as an example. As great as you think retirement may be, it won't make up for thirty-plus years of killing time at jobs you abhor. Instead of waiting until your golden years to really start living your life, begin now, in the present, by seeking out jobs you have a passion for, exploring new hobbies, or taking that exotic vacation you've been dreaming about.

Doing these things in the present will take a significant amount of pressure off of future expectations, since you'll no longer be dependent upon the outcome of those events to make up for lost time. Think of this approach as an effective hedge. The more you can do to enjoy your life right now in the present, the less vulnerable you will be to disappointment from unmet expectations in the future.

Along similar lines, goal setting is an effective way of leveraging the future to implement positive changes in your life today. By mapping out what you want to accomplish, you can track your progress over time and hold yourself accountable for taking action. However, the mistake many people make is thinking that the end goal is the *only* place where happiness and satisfaction can be found.

This kind of mindset does a great disservice to the present by portraying your path to achievement as a constant struggle. Of course, achieving what you set out to do is important, but tying your happiness to the completion of goals can lead to frustration and a lot of hollow victories. What's worse is when you wrongly assume that this hollow feeling can only be remedied by setting more goals, leading you on a path of constant striving with no real enjoyment. Instead, if you focus more on enjoying the ride and rewarding yourself along the way, you'll find that what you gain in the process is much more important than the goals you set out to achieve. It's the journey, not the final destination, that's important in the end.

I used to make all of these lists where I would map out what I wanted to accomplish in the coming weeks, months, and years of my life. This was a highly effective way to get things done, but I eventually found that my lists were way too rigid, and that I really wasn't enjoying the process of accomplishing my goals. If anything, the process felt mechanical, and by the time I would come to the end of my checklist of to-do items, I would be left with a feeling of nothingness and ask myself, "Is this it? Shouldn't I feel happier than this?"

I knew that if I didn't change soon, I'd be spending the rest of my life in a never-ending cycle of goal setting followed by way too brief flashes of enjoyment (relief actually). I eventually realized that the best way I could help myself was to get rid of most of my to-do lists and just focus on what I can do to enjoy my life *right now*. This was, and still is, difficult to achieve. My past behavior of setting rigid goals and struggling to achieve them is such an ingrained part of me. Of course, I still have goals that guide me, but at least now I have a lot more room to be flexible and spontaneous in case anything interesting comes up along the way. Although I still have a long way to go, this shift in philosophy has already opened up many new doors in my life, and helped me to enjoy the ride a great deal more.

WHERE YOU *WILL* FIND HAPPINESS: THE PRESENT

Taking advantage of opportunities to be flexible and spontaneous is one of the best ways to maximize the potential of the present. Being flexible or spontaneous doesn't mean being indecisive or irresponsible. It just means taking advantage of interesting detours in the pursuit of where you'd like to get to in life. Some people seem to have been born with the ability to do this and have no problem capitalizing on unexpected opportunities that life throws their way. Others (myself included) need to learn how to live this way. It's easy to justify not being flexible or spontaneous because those words are usually synonymous with stepping outside of our comfort zones, and that induces fear. Until you are willing to overcome those fears, and drop the notion that you have to follow a fixed plan in life, you'll be denying yourself countless life-changing experiences that the present has to offer.

Another great way to live the present to its fullest is by taking advantage of opportunities for personal growth. We may tell ourselves that (once the timing is right) we will approach that person we've had our eye on, write that book we've been meaning to, or tell that loved one how much we appreciate them. However, concepts like "finding time later," "next time," or "when the timing is right" are only empty promises that may never be realized. Real growth is only achieved by acting now, in the present moment. Every time you don't take advantage of that moment, it will become progressively harder to take action, and there's no guarantee there ever will be a "next time."

Think of the present moment as *the burn*. The burn is analogous to what athletes must fight through if they want to make gains in strength, conditioning, speed, or endurance. If they don't push themselves outside of their comfort zone by consistently training harder than what they're used to, no real progress will be made. Evolving is no different. The only way to make real gains in your personal growth is to take action despite feeling timid, insecure, or fearful. Those difficult moments are where you experience the burn, and without suffering through them, you won't progress. It's easy to imagine all of the great things you're going to do, and all the significant changes you're going to make, while you're sitting comfortably at home sipping on some Pinot Noir. But until you willingly go through the burn of acting on those things in the present moment, it's just idle promises and wishful thinking.

TOMORROW WILL NEVER BE THE SAME

Living the present moment to the fullest is the best gift you could ever give yourself. There will always be ups and downs in life, but those "up" moments can come and go way too quickly if you don't maximize your appreciation of them in the present. We all need to let go of the past that is already gone and the promise of a tomorrow that may never come, because all we are assured of is this moment, and things may never be this perfect again. Tomorrow I could be hit by a car, lose my job, or find out I have cancer. I have absolutely no idea what destiny has in store for me, so my best bet is to live every good moment like it's my last.

One method that helps me do this is spending time at the beginning of each day going over how much *worse* things could be. This may seem counterintuitive, but it's an incredibly effective way of appreciating the present. Too often we spend our time dwelling on what we're lacking, which only winds up devaluing the present and making us feel worse. On the other hand, it's amazing how much better you feel when you're reminded that your life isn't nearly as bad as it could be. As with most self-improvements, the key to implementing this change is to put it into practice every day. You'll have to figure out what works best for you, but I've found that dedicating a few minutes during morning meditation is an effective way to ensure that this practice becomes part of a daily routine.

Some of the most common regrets people have as they near the end of their lives are that they wish they had been more spontaneous, told others how they really felt, didn't waste so much time dwelling on things they had no control of, and just enjoyed the ride wherever it took them.

"If I had my life to live over again, I'd dare to make more mistakes next time. I'd relax. I'd limber up. I'd be sillier than I've been this trip. I would take fewer things seriously. I would take more chances, I would take more trips, I would climb more mountains and swim more rivers. I would eat more ice cream and less beans. I would, perhaps, have more actual troubles but

LIVE IN THE NOW

fewer imaginary ones. You see, I'm one of those people who was sensible and sane, hour after hour, day after day. Oh, I've had my moments. If I had to do it over again, I'd have more of them. In fact, I'd try to have nothing else—just moments, one after another, instead of living so many years ahead of each day."

—Nadine Stair

With this knowledge in mind, what are you going to do now, in the present, to make sure you don't have those same regrets?

LESSON

Too much of our current well-being is affected by time periods that we have no control over. Instead of waiting in vain for a future that may fall short of expectations, or dwelling on a past that's already over and done with, we should focus our attention on what we actually can control: living the present to its fullest. This means throwing away the rigid life plan, taking advantage of opportunities for personal growth, and appreciating how good we have it at all times.

FEAR REGRET, NOT REJECTION

"If only. Those must be the two saddest words in the world."
—Mercedes Lackey

Picture this scenario for a moment. You see the possible girl or guy of your dreams across the room from you. You notice them, they notice you. You smile at each other, and the anticipation builds. You're all set to make your move, but then your heart starts to race, and it feels like your nerves are on fire. Doubts begin to pour into your mind, and you start to question whether the other person is really even interested in you, or if you were just imagining things.

Before you know it, you're frozen in place. You try to placate yourself by saying you'll approach them in the next five minutes. But the longer you wait, the harder it becomes to take action. Finally, the person you've been exchanging longing glances with gets up to leave. They walk by you, giving you one last chance, but all you can muster is a weak smile. Although nothing was said between the two of you, you're both sharing the same thought: *I wonder what could have been.*

You go home that night and bury your head in your pillow, knowing you missed what could have been the chance of a lifetime, all because of the fear of rejection. The regret from your inaction lingers in your mind for days, weeks, or even months. You replay the scenario over and over again in your mind and imagine that you actually do make the approach, and that it's warmly received, but sadly it's too late now. If only you could have that moment back ...

ONE YES CAN OVERCOME A HUNDRED REJECTIONS

It goes without saying that no one enjoys being rejected, whether by a love interest or anyone else. In fact, the fear of rejection relates to any aspect of life where you put yourself at risk of someone saying, "I see what you have to offer, and I'm not interested." But why does this fear of rejection often hold people back from taking their shots at potential happiness, especially when the regret from not acting is much more painful?

The reason can be attributed to our protective, but often misguided, ego. Like a good mother, our ego tries to shield us from the hurt that rejection brings and is unaware that the pain from regret is much worse and lasts much longer. In fact, the fear of rejection is often so exaggerated that it can incite more apprehension in people than heights, public speaking, or even death. In other words, there are some people who would rather die than be rejected! It shouldn't have to be this way.

No one wants to hear that they're unwanted, but you also don't want to deny yourself potential opportunities for happiness by playing it safe all the time. That's why, when contemplating taking a shot at something important to you, it's essential to remind yourself that *regret from not acting will feel worse, and one "yes" makes up for all prior rejections.*

For example, let's say your dream job is to work in television. In order to land one of those highly sought-after positions, there's a very good chance that you'll have to face countless rejections with no guaranteed outcome of success. Such situations leave you with two choices: drop your pursuit in order to avoid the pain of rejection, or press on in spite of it. If you choose to give in to your fears and drop your pursuit prematurely, any initial relief you feel will be far outweighed by the lasting regret of giving up on your dreams. On the other hand, if you decide to press on, you may find that the next company you approach turns out to be the one that is willing to give you a chance. Or maybe it takes five, ten, fifty, or a hundred more rejections before finding someone who is willing to say "yes." The point is it doesn't matter how many "no's" you receive along the way, because once you obtain what you're after—whether it's that dream job or that ideal lover—the pain from *all* prior rejections quickly becomes irrelevant.

DON'T FEAR THE WRONG THING

At the end of your life, wouldn't you rather know that you took your shots at living your best life *in spite of rejection,* rather than missing opportunities because you *feared rejection?* Why deny yourself some of life's greatest opportunities for happiness by being a victim to unnecessary fears? Rejection may affect you for a few minutes, but regret can last a lifetime, so don't fear the wrong thing.

───────────── LESSON ─────────────

No one likes being rejected, but the fear of rejection is often exaggerated and can be an impediment to pursuing potential opportunities for happiness. What you really should fear is the *regret* from not taking your shots at what's important to you, because the pain of regret lasts much longer than any rejection can sting.

LIVE YOUR LIFE
ACCORDING TO TRUTH

"Three things cannot long be hidden: the sun, the moon, and the truth."
—Confucius

Understanding the concept of truth will change the way you view the world, and living by its meaning will improve your well-being considerably. To live according to truth means *recognizing what the right thing to do is in any given situation, and acting accordingly.*

Truth cuts across all aspects of life: relationships, jobs, and even the seemingly mundane decisions we make on a daily basis. We can try to ignore truth because we don't like what it's telling us, but doing so won't make it go away. Any time we ask ourselves, "Am I doing the right thing here?" the answer can always be found in truth.

AN INCONVENIENT TRUTH

People struggle with dilemmas of truth every day. They have a sense that something they're doing (or are contemplating doing) goes against what they believe to be right, yet often ignore this intuition to their own detriment. What many fail to consider is that the conscience has a notoriously long memory, so any disregard for truth is likely to have a lasting negative impact on well-being. This is worth emphasizing: *Your willingness to recognize and act upon truth has a direct impact on your conscience, and ultimately on your well-being.*

For example, it's not uncommon for people to face dilemmas of truth in their jobs, where they're sometimes caught between doing what they're expected to do, and adhering to their conscience. Whether it's a stock-broker being asked to promote a company he knows is bogus, or a soldier being ordered to kill in a war he doesn't believe in, dilemmas of truth often leave no easy choices. Do you disobey your superiors because what you're being asked to do doesn't feel right? Or do you do as you are told, letting the question of whether you acted wrongly simmer in your conscience indefinitely (perhaps all your life)?

There's no doubt that adhering to truth requires a great deal of courage in these kinds of situations, especially considering the pressure to conform to those who control your paycheck. However, it's *you* who will have to live with the consequences of your actions, so you should always ask yourself what will matter more to you in the long run: a pat on the back for a job well done, or a conscience you can sleep with? If the result of your actions leaves you with a heavy conscience, then regardless of what you've gained, it's going to be hard to feel good about yourself when all is said and done.

I don't mention these examples to cast judgment because everybody's situation is different, and everyone has their own idea of what truth means to them. It's up to us as individuals to decide how we handle truth in our lives, because we each have to live with ourselves and the results of our actions.

A CLEAN CONSCIENCE IS A GOOD PILLOW

When I was in my mid-teens, I did what was undoubtedly the dumbest and most regrettable thing of my life. For whatever inexcusable reason, a few friends and I thought it would be fun to break into the house of a disliked classmate who we knew was on vacation. At first we only planned on breaking in so we could play his video games, watch his movies, and eat his junk food. But what started out as a prank turned into a disaster. More friends found out about what we were doing, joined in, and literally trashed the entire house. Eventually this classmate and his family returned to find their home ravaged, their privacy violated, and their possessions in total disarray.

At about this time, it dawned on me how serious of an act I had committed. Not only was it criminal, but I was directly responsible for the pain of others. I became overwhelmed with guilt, and my shameful act wreaked havoc on my adolescent conscience. After a few days of this unbearable mental torture, I finally broke down in front of my mom and owned up to everything. After hearing me out, she calmly told me that I had to do the one thing I feared most, which was to go over to that same house and confess to my classmate and his family what I had done.

I was completely petrified, of course, but deep down I knew it was the truth and the right thing to do, so I did it. Coming clean took a huge weight off of my conscience, and luckily the family was willing to forgive me because I was just a kid. However, I didn't get off that easily. I still had to turn myself in to the police, attend court several times, pay a significant fine, and, as a fifteen-year-old kid in ninth grade, see a probation officer regularly.

Turning myself in like that was one of the hardest things I ever had to do, and took every ounce of courage and humility I had. I knew that by doing it I would completely alienate myself from my friends, be known as a criminal, and, even worse, as a snitch. It's possible that I could have gotten away with what I did by keeping my mouth shut and denying everything, but I have never once doubted that I made the right choice, and I'm thankful to still have a relatively clean conscience.

I can still remember how my grandfather, who was a quintessential tough guy, broke down in tears and told me how proud he was of what

I did. It was a painful lesson to learn on many levels, but it also helped me understand the value of truth, and that it's never too late to do the right thing.

TRUTH IN ACTION

Living your life according to truth doesn't mean you have to live like a saint. Ideally, with enough life experience, you'll have the foresight to recognize truth before acting, but we're all human, and we all make mistakes. What's equally important is how you handle things once you recognize the truth of any misdeeds you've committed.

So take out a pen and paper right now, and write down all of the things you've done in your life that are currently weighing on your conscience. No one else has to see this list but you, so don't hold anything back. Once you've established your list, ask yourself honestly if there is anything you can do to make things right. This includes having the courage and humility to sincerely apologize to anyone you've wronged and offering to make amends, though more may be required.

Even if all you can do is to make a commitment to yourself to live more aligned with truth going forward, at least it's a step in the right direction. I'm not saying this will be easy (it's not), but there's no question it's worth the effort. The more progress you can make toward living your life in harmony with truth, the more your well-being will improve as a result, and the better you will sleep at night.

LESSON

Living your life according to truth means recognizing what the right thing to do is in any given situation, and then having the courage to act appropriately. It would be much easier to just ignore difficult truths and go on with life, but the lasting impact on one's conscience ultimately makes this option self-defeating. Abiding by truth will go a long way toward maintaining a clean conscience and ultimately improving your well-being.

CHOOSE YOUR PASSION,
NOT THE MONEY

"Now what's it to be: The money ... or your life?"
——*A Good Year*

Somewhere along the course of our lives, many of us got the impression that, in order to be happy and successful, we should make as much money as possible. But what no one bothered to mention is that, if we try to achieve happiness through the accumulation of wealth, we would have to put up with jobs that drain our time and energy, stress us out, and leave our lives feeling empty of meaning. And here's the real kicker: unless you're starting out poor, money actually has a negligible effect on well-being anyway! Meanwhile, the pursuit of what we would really love to do gets put off until we're more "financially secure" or "have more time." In other words, never. So why should you delay, even for a second, what you love doing now in order to pursue something that a countless number of older, wiser, and wealthier people have sworn does not make a person any happier?

SUNDAY NIGHT BLUES

How do you feel when you are getting ready for bed on any given Sunday night, knowing you'll soon have to put in a full week of work at a job you loathe? If you're like most people, the answer is: resigned dread. No matter how many fun activities you try to cram into a weekend, it's difficult to evade that unpleasant realization that *yet another* week of passionless work lies ahead. One thing is for sure: you will never reach your full potential this way. When passion is absent from work, your enthusiasm, creativity, and work quality all suffer. Maybe with a constant dose of Starbucks you can manage to get through the work week, but it's a very resistant process.

On the other hand, having a passion for your work maximizes your creativity, energy, and full potential, making everything flow smoothly. We are drawn to people who have passion because their enthusiasm for what they do is extremely convincing and contagious. If you look at any business or occupation, the people who rise to the top and excel are those who have the greatest love for what they do. They are the ones who can spend hour after hour engaged in their work without keeping an eye on the clock. They are the ones willing to do *whatever it takes* to get the best job done without complaining. They are the ones who can come up with creative ideas at any given time since they don't view their work and non-work lives as divorced from each other.

You may have wondered why people who make unimaginable amounts of money don't just retire and enjoy the good life. The reason is that most people who reach that level of wealth are not driven by money. Instead, they are driven by a passion for what they do, and money is just an ancillary benefit. As far as they're concerned, they're already living the good life by doing what they love on a daily basis.

For example, do you think Bill Gates was driven to be the world's richest man when he started out tinkering with computers and developing software? I highly doubt it. He loved what he was doing, believed in it, and invested all of his time and energy into it. We all know what the payoff from his passion was. Steve Jobs, the former iconic CEO of Apple, is another great example of someone who lived his passion and encouraged others to do the same:

"Your work is going to fill a large part of your life, and the only way to be truly satisfied is to do what you believe is great work. And the only way to do great work is to love what you do. If you haven't found it yet, keep looking. Don't settle. As with all matters of the heart, you'll know when you find it. And, like any great relationship, it just gets better and better as the years roll on." [2]

PASSION IS CONTAGIOUS

Keep in mind that fulfilling a passion doesn't have to mean starting your own company, writing a symphony, or entering the Peace Corps. By just pursuing what you love to do (whatever that may be), you will be bringing a great deal of energy and enthusiasm into the world, making it a better place for you and everyone you come into contact with.

A number of years ago I worked with a client, JB, who was extremely passionate about his job. He was an entrepreneur who invested most of his time, energy, and money into his company. JB was very successful and made more than enough money to live comfortably, but it wasn't always that way. He spent a lot of time facing rejection, living off of very little money, and even having to sell off most of his assets—all to pursue a passion that he believed in. He could have easily taken the safe road at any point to save himself the discomfort, but he had the courage of his convictions. His patience and persistence eventually paid off to the point where he was able to pursue his passion *and* make good money in the process.

I'll never forget the day we went out to dinner with a potential big-time customer for JB's business. We were all ravenous after a long day preparing for the meeting, so when the food finally arrived, I went to work on immediately devouring my prime rib. To my surprise, I looked over and saw that JB had barely touched his plate. Instead of licking his plate clean like I was doing, he was so engrossed in a conversation with this customer that he had actually forgotten to eat! I watched him talk about his company

---

2 Steve Jobs, Stanford University Commencement, 2005

with so much passion and enthusiasm that I couldn't see how anybody would not believe in his business.

I was so inspired by that dinner that I had an epiphany. I made a promise to myself that from that day forward I would only pursue work that had the potential to inspire at least an inkling of the passion I had witnessed in JB that night. I mean, what was the point of giving my time and energy to work that, when I was honest with myself, I could really care less about? I wanted to feel that passion, creativity, and energy in my work the way JB did. Anything less would be cheating myself.

IT DOESN'T MEAN YOU HAVE TO BE BROKE

A problem you may run into trying to adhere to this lesson is that we often have conflicting values. We want to do what we love, but we also want money to pay the bills, buy nice things, and secure the future. I'm not disagreeing with the fact that having money is a very necessary part of life, but making money and following your passion do not have to be mutually exclusive. Instead of choosing between the two, find a way to make money *by* pursuing your passion.

For some, that's easier than for others. Some people just know from an early age that they want to pursue a career in music, art, teaching, or business, while others (myself included) require more self-analysis to discover what they'd truly love to do with their lives. Either way, the goal is to find something where the line between your everyday work and non-work life is as blurred as possible.

I've found that one useful way of doing this is to look at what you spend the majority of your free time on, as well as what gives you the most enjoyment. We all tend to do things we enjoy when we have the opportunity, so there is usually a significant overlap between the two.

The next step is to make a list of all those interests, then research any potential jobs or schooling that can be leveraged to pursue them. There is usually more than one way to arrive at the same destination, and nothing should be ruled out, including starting your own business if the job you're looking for does not yet exist.

I used to think I had no real passion for anything. At best I thought I had hobbies with little potential to make a living out of, but I was wrong. Once I took a deeper look at what I was doing with my free time, I realized I had several true passions that could be linked to future careers. For starters, I loved to travel and would do so at any given opportunity, so that was certainly a passion. I would try to work out every day and got pleasure out of feeling healthy, so wellness was something else I loved. Anytime I would watch TV it was mostly for something sports-related, so there was another. Finally, I knew that any time I helped someone I would get a rush of good feelings, so helping people was another potential passion I could pursue.

After going through this exercise, it quickly dawned on me that there was absolutely nothing preventing me from pursuing a job in travel, health, sports, or self-help. There were tons of positions related to those industries that I could pursue as a career. Maybe it wasn't the traditional path I had once envisioned, but at least I would be happy doing something I loved.

CHOOSE PASSION OVER PAYCHECK

Deciding to pursue a passion full time is never an easy decision. Most of us are dissuaded from doing so because it's certain to take us out of our comfort zone, and that scares us. We allow ourselves to be convinced (by ourselves or others) that future success is just too uncertain, so we accept that uninspiring corporate job with a steady paycheck and good benefits.

If you do decide to follow your passion (which I sincerely hope you do), you'll need to have the courage of your convictions, and a bit of a thick skin. For instance, when you first start out, you will likely be surrounded by people who make a lot more money than you do, working at conventional jobs that you're completely capable of doing yourself. This may lead you to feel like you're missing out on something, but don't be fooled by that illusion. Remember, more money is not the goal here, it's more happiness, and choosing to do what you love will *always* lead to the greater happiness.

─── LESSON ───

When choosing a career, the payoff in terms of happiness and success will be far greater if you pursue your passion over money. The stress and anguish that result from working at an uninspiring job are very real, and only remedied by work that frees your creative spirit, boosts your energy level, and ignites your strongest passions.

7

ALWAYS LEAVE A WINNER

"Quitting while you're ahead is not the same as quitting."
—*American Gangster*

The world is full of choices, and it's easy to be overwhelmed by them all. If we don't have a sound strategy to help us navigate the thousands of options we face on a daily basis, we're likely to become entangled in drawn-out searches that leave us feeling exhausted and unsatisfied. Even when we're fortunate enough to find what we're looking for—at the mall or in life—we often press on anyway, seduced by the allure of new possibilities and unexamined choices. Unfortunately, you're unlikely to end up happy this way. On the other hand, when you learn to walk away a winner, you'll find life to be much more satisfying.

UNEXAMINED CHOICES
SHOULD BE LEFT UNEXAMINED

One of the biggest impediments to walking away a winner is the ability to ignore unexamined choices. In *The Paradox of Choice*, Barry Schwartz talks about this challenge when describing what he calls *satisficers* and *maximizers*. Satisficers are consumers who have a certain criteria in mind when looking to buy anything like food, clothing, or gifts. Once they find something that meets their criteria, they make the purchase and look no further. As far as they're concerned, they've accomplished what they set out to do and can leave feeling satisfied. In contrast, maximizers tend to be much more obsessive-compulsive. They will continue to shop until they have explored all possible options and are convinced they have made the best possible purchase.

It should be easy to draw a parallel between shopping and that of more profound life choices. Of course we always want to make the best choices for ourselves at all times, but does the extra time and effort justify outcomes that may only make us marginally happier, if at all? No according to Schwartz, who argues convincingly that it's the constant searching and multiple choices that actually make maximizers *less* happy in the end, because they tend to dwell on whether or not there is something (or someone) better out there that they may have missed.

> "If you're a satisficer, the number of available options need not have a significant impact on your decision making. When you examine an object and it's good enough to meet your standards, you look no further; thus, the countless other available choices become irrelevant. But if you're a maximizer, every option has the potential to snare you into endless tangles of anxiety, regret, and second-guessing."[3]

What usually deters people from becoming a satisficer is the fear that they're going to miss out on a better deal tomorrow, in another store, or

---

3 Barry Schwartz, *The Paradox of Choice*

at another bar. The irony is that those other options only become relevant if you allow them to be, so the idea is to not seek them out.

In order to avoid being a maximizer and getting bogged down by a myriad of options, establish a list of criteria in advance of whatever it is you're searching for. This list could be something you keep in a journal, a wallet, or even just your mind, as long as it's readily accessible. Once that list is established, practice the discipline of walking away a winner once you find what you're seeking. Even if that means starting small with a routine trip to the mall or supermarket, get used to being a satisficer, and then work your way up to practicing this principle with more profound life decisions. Having been a maximizer for most of my life, I can personally attest that learning to live as a satisficer provides far greater contentment, and is well worth the effort.

TAKE THE MONEY AND RUN!

I used to be a pretty big gambler in college. Whether it was betting on sports, blackjack, or anything else, I loved the high I would get from having a stake in the game. An otherwise snoozer of a college football matchup between North Dakota State and Southern Utah could turn into a thrilling heart stopper if I had money on the line. In fact, it was not uncommon for me to spend entire weekends betting on games until, inevitably, I would either break even or lose money.

After blowing through most of my paltry savings this way, I began to think about why I was even gambling in the first place. I knew I enjoyed gambling and occasionally making free money, but even when I was winning, I would always bet more. It finally occurred to me that I had an insatiable desire to win as much as possible without any defined goal. It wasn't like I was saying to myself, "I really need $200 so I can buy an iPhone, so once I win $200 I will stop." As silly as that sounds, that would have made a lot more sense than what I was doing.

So instead of allowing my enjoyment of gambling to become a bottomless drain on my time and finances, I decided I needed to have a certain limit in mind and the discipline to walk away once that point was reached.

Now anytime I casually gamble, I establish self-imposed limitations that work perfectly well. For example, if I am up or down, say, a hundred dollars, I stop no questions asked. If I lose the hundred dollars, then I consider it an entertainment expense that I can live with. If I am up a hundred dollars, then I am that much richer for having done practically nothing. Maybe a hundred dollars isn't a whole lot of money, but I know from experience that winning a hundred dollars does not feel all that different from winning, say, two hundred dollars. What *does* feel different (worse actually) is when I wind up with less money because I didn't walk away when I had the chance.

I use gambling as an example, but walking away a winner is relevant to more important areas of life as well, such as choosing a life partner. I had always believed that, if I ever met someone who had just enough of the qualities I was seeking (attractive, kind, trustworthy), then I would strongly consider leaving my single life as a winner. Similar to my dilemma with gambling, I had a sense that a continued search for that undefined *perfect* woman would ultimately leave me with nothing and no one.

Thankfully I became aware of this lesson before meeting my beautiful and loving wife, who has allowed me to walk away an incredibly happy winner. But it does make me wonder how many other people had that right person to walk away with at some point in their lives, but passed it up in order to try (in vain) to find someone *more perfect*. By saying this, I'm certainly not recommending that you settle for less than what you think you deserve. My point is that it's important to recognize when what you have in front of you has a high probability of making you happy—and when that's the case, to be disciplined enough to "take the money and run."

LESSON

Whether it's gambling on blackjack, shopping at the mall, or choosing your spouse, the way to give yourself great odds for reaching contentment is the same: establish what you want, stick to the criteria you have in mind, and walk away a winner once you find what you are seeking.

EVERYTHING HAPPENS FOR A REASON
(EVEN IF YOU DON'T KNOW WHAT IT IS!)

*"I do not believe in fate that falls on men however they act;
but I do believe in fate that falls on them unless they act."*
—G.K. Chesterton

"Everything happens for a reason" is a saying we hear a lot, usually from someone trying to help us find a positive upside in an otherwise unfavorable situation. That person may just be saying this to us out of habit, but they are giving us great advice: everything *does* happen for a reason, even if we don't know what that reason is at the time. No matter what the context is, if you look at everything with the idea that some good or potential for good is imbedded in it, then otherwise-negative events will be perceived in a more favorable light. What has happened is already done, so we should always look for ways in which unchangeable past events can benefit us going forward. On the other hand, if we take the position of being helpless victims anytime something bad happens, then we will suffer unnecessarily.

EVERY CRISIS IS AN OPPORTUNITY

Are you depressed because you got laid off from your steady but uninspiring job? Maybe greater happiness is waiting for you in another field of work and now this is the opportunity to pursue it. Are you sad because your boyfriend or girlfriend broke up with you, even though you weren't that into them? Maybe you'll run into the true love of your life on your next vacation, a trip you wouldn't have considered taking if you were still tied down.

The point of these examples is that you just don't know what's going to happen as a result of different life events, so why allow yourself to suffer unnecessarily because of them? It doesn't matter whether or not you can see the reason behind what happens to you, *it's how you frame unchangeable events* that matters. When it comes down to it, you really have two alternatives: you can look at negative events as random occurrences and feel like a helpless victim, or look at negative events as having occurred for some reason and embrace what lies ahead for you as a result.

Every lesson I have learned, whether through negative or positive events, was necessary for my personal development in some way, and led me to where I am today. Having this perspective has brought me so much contentment and makes me feel in touch with the flow of life. But that was not always the case. Like others, I used to fight hard against the negative events that occurred in my life, and I suffered tremendously because of it.

When I was a teenager in high school, the main thing that concerned me (aside from losing my virginity, of course) was fitting in with the cool crowd. My academics took a far backseat to my social pursuits, and as a result my grades dropped off precipitously. For someone who had always excelled in school, I was heading in the completely wrong direction. I was close to failing in a few subjects, got drunk on a regular basis, and even quit the wrestling team. My chances of entering into a top university were falling more and more by the wayside each day, but it didn't matter to me at the time. As long as I was hanging out with the cool kids, then everything would be fine, or so I thought.

High school cliques being as fickle as they are, one day I found myself on the outside looking in, and was no longer considered cool. In an instant

I had lost all my friends and felt completely alone. When you're a teenager, losing your friends can seem as if your whole world has fallen apart, as I felt mine had. I was supposed to be having the time of my life, but instead I was wallowing in deep depression. Since I now had lots of free time on my hands and no one to spend it with, I reluctantly began to refocus on my studies. This was by no means a voluntary choice, but one born out of a lack of options.

As all of this was happening to me, I rebelled against my reality by being depressed and wishing more than anything to be cool again. I wasn't aware of it at the time, but everything was happening to me in that way for a reason: to put me on a new path of positive growth and happiness. All of the studying I did with my unexpected free time helped me get into a top university, something that seemed out of the question only a year prior. In time, that accomplishment allowed me to have an unforgettable college experience, receive a great education, and meet the *real* friends I still have today.

When I look back on that experience, I am so thankful things played out the way they did, despite the fact that I resisted what was happening at the time. Now I know better than to resist what life hands me by getting down or stuck in place. Instead, I remind myself that whatever happens to me happens with good reason, even if I don't know what the reason is yet. Embracing this optimistic perspective certainly beats the alternative of suffering unnecessarily.

GOOD FORTUNE FOLLOWS ACTION

To be clear, believing that everything happens for a reason isn't just about Pollyanna optimism. If you want to find out what new opportunities for growth and happiness life is nudging you toward, real action is required.

For instance, instead of sitting at home discouraged because you've lost your job, you could take advantage of that time to acquire any useful skills that you're lacking, and make yourself more valuable to future employers. Instead of moping around heartbroken because of a failed relationship, you could use the pain of that breakup as an impetus to learn from any mistakes you've made, and improve yourself as a person for when someone special comes along. In fact, instead of resisting any kind of difficult period in your life, focus on what you can do *now* to pull yourself out of that down cycle.

Whatever you do, don't just sit around depressed waiting for the fates to smile upon you. Fortune favors the bold and the hard-working, and there is no better time to motivate yourself than when your back is against the wall. Give the negative events in your life meaning by taking control of your destiny through action.

> "Do we cringe before our destiny, feeling sorry for ourselves, crying out: If only we could have been such and such? If so we shall go down like cowards or, more likely, robots—mechanical human beings whom the universe erases. Or do we confront destiny directly, using it as a stimulus to call forth our best efforts, our greatest sensitivity, our sharpest creative vision? If so, we then are men and women for whom the future cries."
>
> —Rollo May, *Freedom and Destiny*

--------------------- LESSON ---------------------

Everything that happens to you in life occurs for some reason, even if you don't know what that reason is at the time. Instead of allowing negative life events to turn you into a helpless victim, reframe them as new opportunities for growth and happiness that spur you into action.

CHOOSE YOUR SURROUNDINGS CAREFULLY

*"If you surround yourself with good people, you'll go far.
If you start hanging out with knuckleheads, you'll be right in the
knucklehead section the rest of your life."*
—Kid Rock

The kind of people you choose to surround yourself with says a lot about who you are, how you view the world, and the person you aspire to be. If you want to reach your full potential in this life, make a conscious effort to surround yourself with individuals you can learn from, and who help elevate you to higher levels of growth and personal development. The more time you're able to spend with people who act as a positive influence on your life, the more likely you are to conform to their behavior. Unfortunately, the same can be said of those who serve as a negative influence, so be sure to choose your companions carefully.

LET THE POSITIVE QUALITIES OF OTHERS RUB OFF ON YOU

Humbly acknowledging that you could use the help of others isn't a sign of weakness, it's a sign of strength. Henry Ford was known for saying how he wasn't smart enough to know everything, but smart enough to know the right people he could call on to tell him anything he needed to know. The same concept applies to how you should view your own personal development. If you lack certain qualities that you'd like to possess, surround yourself with people who can help you cultivate them. Even if you're capable of developing those qualities on your own over time, why not facilitate the process by learning from people who have something relatable to teach you?

The first step in putting this plan into practice is to make a list of all the qualities you feel you're lacking and would like to develop further. Examples could include generosity, spontaneity, courage, discipline, confidence, health, or anything else that's important to you. Once you've established what you'd like to improve about yourself, make a list of all the people—family members, friends, acquaintances, role models—whom you believe possess those particular traits, and then humbly ask for their help.

You don't have to limit yourself to just people you already know; it can be anybody you look up to. Throughout my life I've reached out to, and sought the guidance of, several well-known authors, professors, athletes, and business leaders—none of whom I had ever spoken to previously. To my pleasant surprise, most of them responded quickly, were generous with their time, and provided invaluable advice.

The next step is to find a way to spend more time with these individuals so that their positive characteristics can rub off on you. Ideally you could find out how they came to possess the particular qualities that you desire to incorporate in yourself. Does it just come naturally to them, or do they have to work at it? Were these qualities passed on to them from someone *they* were influenced by, or did they develop them on their own?

The final step is to emulate these desired qualities in your own life. Try your best to act the way they act, think the way they think, and even feel the way they feel, while exhibiting the desired behaviors.

This will take plenty of time and effort on your part, but with enough practice and patience, you'll eventually be able to assimilate these qualities into your own persona, and will be much better for it. Surrounding yourself with people you want to emulate is a strong way to approach life, because there is always more you can learn, and you can always be growing.

YOUR SURROUNDINGS TELL A LOT ABOUT YOU

Sadly there are those who like to take a different approach. Instead of relying on people they admire to help push them to higher levels of personal development, they try to stand out by surrounding themselves with people they consider to be inferior in some way. Unlike surrounding yourself with people who you can learn from, this kind of mentality offers very limited opportunities for personal growth, and you only wind up conforming down to those you had hoped to stand out from.

In a lot of ways, who you surround yourself with says a lot about how you view the world. If you only surround yourself with inferior people just to make yourself look better, it's as if you view the world as a zero-sum game, where someone else's success is seen as a threat to your own. On the other hand, if you constantly surround yourself with thriving people who possess enviable qualities that you lack, it's as if you believe that success breeds success, and that the positive attributes of others can improve your own life.

> "Those we choose to spend time with define both who we think we are and who we want to be. They must be chosen carefully."
>
> —Gordon Livingston, *How to Love*

BE RIGOROUS ABOUT YOUR SURROUNDINGS

Not only is it important to surround yourself with people you can learn from, but if you want to live your best life, you should never conform to those who influence you in any negative way. Examples of negative influences are ubiquitous, and can include overt behaviors such as acting reckless, stealing, and abusing drugs or alcohol. It can also include more subtle, but not necessarily less negative, behaviors such as lying, complaining, and acting selfish.

Spending time with people who exhibit these types of negative characteristics may be difficult to avoid due to work, family obligations, or a living situation, and if you're not careful, you may start to believe that those behaviors are okay because *they're doing it.* That's why it's important to always be aware of your environment and the people you spend time with, lest the wrong ones rub off on you.

When I was younger, I used to be intimidated by anyone who possessed the kinds of admirable traits that I lacked. Instead of seeking out their help and advice, I chose to avoid them, feeling safer and more comfortable in a group of friends who, despite being decent enough people, never pushed me in any positive way or helped me grow. I was even hesitant to break ties with people who had a clear negative influence on my life, fearing they would take offense to my desire to spend less time with them. Eventually I realized that, if I was ever going to develop into the person I aspired to be, I needed to be a lot more selective about who I hung out with.

Now I am rigorous when it comes to the people I surround myself with, and have deliberately scaled back the amount of time I spend with those who were influencing me in any negative way—including colleagues, friends, and even some family members. It's not that I'm cold hearted or antisocial, I just desperately want to reach my full potential in this life, and consciously choose to be around those who will help bring that out in me. There's no question that making this change has paid off enormously in my development, and thanks to my new companions, I've learned to be more generous, overcome more fears, live healthier, and become a better man. But my work is not done. There is still so much more I can learn, and I have plenty of room to grow.

Take a second to look around you. Do the people you surround yourself with provide a positive influence on your life? Are they helping you develop the kind of qualities that make you a better human being? If not, it may be time to re-evaluate some of those relationships and make some changes. Reaching your full potential in life takes a great deal of work, but is made significantly easier by surrounding yourself with people who bring out the best in you.

LESSON

The kind of people you surround yourself with says a lot about who you are, how you view the world, and what you want to become. If you want to ascend to higher levels of growth and personal development, make an effort to seek out the guidance, wisdom, and influence of those who possess the positive qualities that you're lacking—individuals who can help you realize your greatest potential.

DON'T BE A SLAVE
TO YOUR GENES

Make $ › secure mate › reproduce = genes happy
(but are YOU happy?)

We all possess certain hard-wired behavior patterns that help us to survive and reproduce. This hard-wiring (located in our genes) has been molded throughout the history of human evolution and influences our behavior daily. Most of the time the goals of our genes are in sync with our desires, so we rarely give it a second thought. Eating feels good when we're hungry, resting feels good when we're tired, and sex feels good when ... well, just about any time!

The reason we feel good is because all of these behaviors are helping us in some way to survive or reproduce (the two main goals of our genes), so our genes reward us with pleasurable feelings. This evolved system of positive reinforcement ensures that these behaviors carry on indefinitely, and that life continues to thrive.

Unfortunately, there are times when the goals of our genes are not in perfect harmony with our own personal aspirations, and we are left vulnerable to the consequences. At first glance this seems illogical because our genes need us to survive, and one would assume they should always be acting in our best interest. The explanation can be found in the fact that our genes do not evolve at the same rate society evolves at—meaning that what worked for our ancestors may not work so well for us in this day and age. Consequently, until our genes catch up and adapt to present-day circumstances, there will always be some disconnect between what's best for them and what's best for us.

THE GORDON GECKO SYNDROME

During the time of our hunter-gatherer ancestors, men were the exclusive providers, and the currency they sought was food (the equivalent of money in today's world). The more food you could successfully hunt and gather translated into greater chances of survival and reproduction.

Nowadays, the impulse to accumulate food (money) is not nearly as relevant. Besides the fact that women are equally capable of being providers themselves, men do not need an excess of food or money to ensure they will survive, reproduce, and be happy. But since physical evolution is slow to catch on, our genes still perceive that our survival is tenuous, so we continue feeling the urge to secure as many resources as we can gather. We are essentially fooled into thinking that, no matter how much we have, we still need more, and as a result our personal well-being suffers from a lack of contentment.

It took me several years of high-stress, ruined relationships, and eventually a quarter-life crisis to see the folly of my own personal pursuit of money. Despite a high-paying salary, I finally came to the conclusion that striving to earn more money wasn't worth the trouble if my health, relationships, and overall well-being were going to suffer. For most of my life I didn't even have a clear idea of what I was making money for, I just knew I needed to make it, *or else!* Or else what? I would starve and die single and lonely? My genes may have been under that assumption, but that was certainly not my reality.

The way to avoid being a slave to this outdated genetic impulse starts with having a clear idea of what you are actually making money for (write it out if you have to). Is it more things or a super-sized bank account that you are after? Or is it less stress, more free time, and greater happiness? If it's the latter, make sure there is no disconnect between those aspirations and your current behavior. For example, if you find that you're working yourself into the ground, despite having more than enough financial resources to already live comfortably, then you may want to rethink your priorities.

At best, money is just an intermediary step to some greater end. At worst it can lead to all sorts of problems that distract you from what your real aspirations are. Instead of making your life more complicated than it needs to be, always have the end goal in mind, and pursue what you're really after in the first place.

FORGETTING YOUR RAINCOAT

Your genes not only want to survive during your lifetime, but they aspire to be passed on to future generations as well. The only way they can do that is if you reproduce. During sex, our genes perceive that we are in the process of reproducing, so we are rewarded with a flood of intoxicating chemicals that make us feel really, *really* good. However, if we let this potent feeling get the best of us and fail to use proper protection, it can lead to significant unintended consequences.

We may think that unprotected sex feels so good and natural that it justifies not wearing protection, but what feels so good in a brief flash of ecstasy will be long forgotten when the reality of an unplanned pregnancy or STD hits home. I've often heard people complain about how wearing a condom is clumsy, and just doesn't feel as good as going au natural. This is an understandable point of view, but when you take a second to think about how much time, commitment, and resources go into raising a child, putting a condom on doesn't seem like much of a sacrifice. Along the same lines, an STD can be embarrassing, costly, and sometimes very serious, so the marginal extra pleasure simply doesn't justify the risk.

Unless you're trying to become a parent or don't mind an awkward visit to the doctor, the easiest way to avoid these consequences is straightforward: be properly prepared and use protection at all times. It doesn't matter if you swear to yourself that you have no intention of having sex, it never hurts to be overly prepared *just in case*. Preventative measures like condoms and other forms of birth control are not a hundred percent effective a hundred percent of the time, but they do offer a very safe option. That's why it's necessary to prepare yourself beforehand, when you're clearheaded and able to make rational decisions. It's much harder to act rationally in the heat of the moment when the forces urging you to consummate are at their strongest, as Dan Ariely confirmed through various studies on decision making and sexual arousal:

> "One thing is sure: if we don't teach our young people how to deal with sex when they are half out of their minds, we are not only fooling them; we're fooling ourselves as well. Whatever lessons we teach them, we need to help them understand that they will react differently when they are calm and cool from when their hormones are raging at fever pitch (and of course the same also applies to our own behavior)." [4]

BUNDLES OF JOY

Speaking of becoming a parent, an almost universal belief is that having kids is something everyone *ought* to do. Since the survival of our genes depends on us reproducing, it's no coincidence that this assumption is deeply imbedded in most people. I'm not saying that children can't provide immense joy, but you should be fully aware of what you are getting

---

4 Dan Ariely, *Predictably Irrational*

yourself into before making presumptions about their effect on your future well-being.

At a minimum, having children changes your life significantly. I'm not just talking about having to wake up in the middle of the night to cuddle or feed them. I'm talking about the fact that there is now at least one person in your life you have to think about before yourself. That can be a good thing, an experience that teaches you greater love and selflessness. But it's a lifelong commitment (through good times and bad) of love, resources, energy, and time.

My brother, who was thirty-two and living with my mom at the time, once made a joke that summed up this sentiment perfectly: "Make sure you know what you are getting yourself into when you decide to have kids, because even thirty-two years later, you could still be feeding them and giving them a place to live!" My mom agreed whole-heartedly.

Before just assuming that having kids is something you ought to do, ask yourself if you are honestly prepared for the commitment and sacrifice that is needed to raise a child. This will help you avoid regrets down the road, such as: "I wish I would have traveled more, taken that one job, or just waited longer."

Go over this with yourself and with your spouse *before* having kids. Is there anything in your life right now that you really want to accomplish before having children? Does your spouse want to have kids before you are ready to? Whatever the hesitation, make sure you are making the decision with the full knowledge of what you are getting into. Then, if and when you do decide to have children, you will be prepared for it, and welcome it.

Being a parent can be an incredibly rewarding experience on so many levels. But it is not a decision that should be taken lightly, and certainly not one that should be decided by genetic impulses alone.

———————————————— LESSON ————————————————

Whether it's pursuing money to no end or the urge to have unprotected sex, humans have evolved certain hard-wired behaviors that don't always serve our current best interests. Fortunately, you don't have to be a slave to these impulses. The key is recognizing when your intrinsic motives don't align with your personal aspirations, then using this knowledge to plan ahead and make smart decisions about what serves *your* best interest, not the best interest of outdated genetic impulses.

STAND UP FOR YOURSELF 11

"Courage is fire, and bullying is smoke."
—Benjamin Disraeli

First impressions count for a lot, and standing up for yourself when warranted sets an important precedent for what someone should expect from you. When you don't stand up for yourself in the face of bullying or harassment, people will presume that you're weak, and won't hesitate to take advantage of you. You may have been taught to take the high road or to just turn the other cheek, but those solutions, although noble, usually don't fix the problem. On the other hand, having the courage to stand up for yourself (with your words *and* your actions) sends a clear message that you're no pushover, and that you won't be taken advantage of without a fight.

BULLIES BEWARE

Let's take a hypothetical example and say there's a bully at your school who's threatening to kick your ass if you don't hand over your lunch money, do his homework, or help him cheat. If you give in thinking that it will appease him (or her), guess what? He'll come back tomorrow with the same threats, but even more confidence. This cycle will likely go on indefinitely, as he will have pegged you as someone weak whom he can take advantage of whenever he chooses.

Instead of relying on more appeasement to solve the problem, the best way to break this cycle is to never let it begin in the first place. By summoning the courage to stand up for yourself right from the get-go, you'll be sending an unambiguous signal that you have no intention of succumbing to threats from *anyone,* ever. Even if that means having to take a few lumps in the short-term, you'll still come out ahead in the long run by getting the bully to respect your tenacity and leave you be.

When you think about it from the bully's perspective, they're not going to want to keep harassing you if they think you're always going to put up a struggle. They'll think it's too much work for them, especially given the fact that there are other, weaker people out there that they can torment without similar resistance.

Bullying takes on many different forms and isn't limited to the prototypical brute who tries to intimidate you with the threat of force. It also includes the over-demanding boss who keeps you working late every night, the controlling spouse who doesn't want you to have a life of your own, and the overbearing family member who makes you feel guilty for not rushing to their every need. Regardless of who is doing the bullying, the moral is always the same: if you don't stand up for yourself, you will be taken advantage of.

DIARY OF A WIMPY KID

I was picked on a lot when I was younger because I was small, had few real friends, and would never stand up for myself. Not surprisingly, some people took advantage of that. On numerous occasions I was pushed around, smacked up, and even spit on, yet never did anything to defend myself. It's no wonder the harassment went on for so long. The guys who were bullying me quickly found out I would never put up a fight, and knew they had free reign to do what they pleased.

I also remember how much of a pushover I was with my first serious girlfriend. I tolerated a lot of behavior that I shouldn't have, and the only real stand I ever took was to make empty threats that I would never follow through on. This pattern continued until she eventually broke up with me. Back then I thought I was placating her by tolerating her behavior, but I realize now it was my not taking a stand that led her to lose respect for me.

I contrast those experiences with how I live my life now, and the difference is astounding. Having gained the nerve to stand up for myself, this once debilitating feeling of weakness has been transformed into something positive, and I no longer fear being taken advantage of. Whether I'm dealing with friends, family members, or even bullies, this new approach has not only resulted in more mutually respectful relationships, but has vastly improved my own self-respect as well.

SENDING THE RIGHT MESSAGE

There are numerous real-world situations where standing up for yourself is required. If it's a family member who always comes looking for a handout, standing up for yourself could mean not succumbing to unwarranted guilt by refusing to bail them out. If it's a romantic partner who treats you poorly, it could mean sending a clear message that you have no intention of staying in a relationship where a person acts like that. If it's a bully who tries to take advantage of you in some way, it could mean a determination to stand your ground and demonstrating that you have no intention of ever backing down.

There's no question that standing up for yourself in these situations requires a strong backbone, because no one wants to voluntarily alienate a loved one, lose a partner, or risk a potential confrontation. However, the problem is that doing nothing can sub-communicate tolerance of an unwanted behavior, and that's not in your best interest. It's ironic, but standing up for yourself actually results in healthier, more balanced relationships with the people who are troubling you.

Most importantly, have the courage of your convictions any time you stand up for yourself, and be willing to back up your words with action. If not, people will quickly figure out that your threats hold little weight, and won't be discouraged from taking further advantage of you. It's also imperative that you stand up for yourself sooner rather than later, because doing so becomes progressively less effective once that initial window of opportunity has closed. If people become used to getting what they want from you without resistance, they'll be much more reluctant to alter their behavior going forward.

> "Freedom once granted will not be relinquished without a fight."
>
> —Robert Cialdini, *Influence*

CHOOSE YOUR BATTLES WISELY

Lastly, it's important to point out that not every situation necessitates taking a stand. You only need to stand up for yourself when it's warranted, and when not doing so could lead to recurring consequences. The goal here is to be strong and courageous, not confrontational or hypersensitive.

It also goes without saying that you should avoid standing up for yourself when doing so puts you in any kind of serious danger (unless it's something worth risking your life over). A few years ago I was held up at knifepoint on a beach in South America. Instead of standing up for myself, I was more than happy to graciously hand over my iPod, money, and shoes to the armed thugs, without hesitation. I knew that my life was potentially at stake, and that standing up for myself in that situation would not only have been extremely foolish, but completely pointless.

LESSON

There will always be people in life who try to take advantage of you if given the opportunity. Standing up for yourself helps ensure that doesn't happen. Whether it's holding your ground in the face of a bully or refusing to tolerate poor treatment in a relationship, standing up for yourself is most effective when done early, and with the courage of your convictions.

12
CONSIDER ADAPTATION

"In general, human beings are remarkably bad at predicting
how various experiences will make them feel."
—Barry Schwartz, *The Paradox of Choice*

I first learned about the concept of adaptation from reading *The Paradox of Choice*, a book I consider a must-read. The basic premise of adaptation is that, no matter how great our initial excitement is about certain things or events in life, we will eventually adapt to our new circumstances and return to a baseline level of happiness.

This ubiquitous feature of human psychology helps explain why material possessions don't have a lasting effect on our happiness, why we don't stay madly in love forever, and why we are generally poor judges of how current decisions will affect us in the future. Although adaptation is not something that can be avoided, a proper understanding of how it can affect you will go a long way toward making better life choices.

BUYER BEWARE

It makes sense that we would possess an attribute like adaptation. After all, we live in an ever-changing environment where we are continuously bombarded by information and stimuli. If everything always seemed "new" to us, we would feel overwhelmed all the time; so we need the ability to continuously adapt. But even though adaptation allows us to cope with our surroundings better, it can also dampen our excitement about things that we wish *would* keep our interest longer, such as those material possessions we spend our hard-earned money on.

For example, let's say you're contemplating buying a nice new foreign car, like a BMW. Although it will set you back financially, you anticipate that owning a new BMW will give you a pleasurable feeling every time you coast down the highway, pull in to work, or see it gleaming in your driveway. However, a few months down the road, you will begin to adapt to that new BMW which, by then, will not seem so new anymore. What was once a symbol of so much pride and pleasure is now seen as just a means of transport. Eventually, you will feel no different than if you had bought a less expensive, but equally reliable, car. The only *real* difference is that you'll be thousands of dollars poorer.

To make this example more personal, try to think back to all of those pricey "things" you were so desperate to have at one point in your life—that new designer purse, fancy Swiss watch, or high-tech gizmo—and then think about where they are now. Do they still give you that warm, fuzzy feeling like they did when you first bought them? Or are they collecting dust somewhere? In all likelihood, those costly material possessions have had a negligible effect on your well-being for some time now, so it's fair to ask yourself whether, in retrospect, they were worth all that money.

I'm not saying you shouldn't treat yourself to nice material things, especially if you can easily afford them. The point is to be aware that adaptation is real and will eventually take effect, so it's worth considering whether the cost justifies the future benefit, especially given other, less expensive alternatives.

Losing enthusiasm for high-priced material possessions is one thing, but sometimes the effects of adaptation can have much more permanent consequences. For instance, when I was in college I had the ingenious idea of getting a tattoo of an Italian flag on my shoulder. I was, after all, a hundred percent Italian, so it seemed to make a lot of sense at the time. So, on a whim, I went to a tattoo parlor and had it done. I remember thinking I would love this tattoo forever because I was proudly Italian and always would be! During the first few weeks, when the tattoo was still nice and fresh, I would pull my sleeve up when no one was looking and check out my shoulder in the mirror. "Man that looks cool!" I would say to myself, quite pleased with my decision.

However, as the months went by and adaptation started to set in, I became less and less enamored with my tattoo. I would see it at least once a day when I was getting ready to shower and would either ignore it completely or wonder aloud why I decided to get this multi-colored ink permanently engraved on my body. It's not that I was any less proud of my heritage; it's just that I felt silly having a tattooed flag of a country I had never even been to. For a while it was difficult to acknowledge that I had made such a mistake, so I tried to convince myself (falsely) that I was happy with my decision. But over time I began to accept that this tattoo wasn't congruent with who I was, and I eventually decided to have it covered up with something more neutral.

Looking back on it now, I realize my biggest error was thinking that the initial feeling of "cool" that I got from my tattoo would last forever. I was projecting how I felt in the present onto the future without considering the likely impact of adaptation, which in the case of things like tattoos, can have permanent consequences.

'TIL ADAPTATION DO US PART

If adaptation is relevant to decisions about material possessions and (ahem) Italian flag tattoos, what about something more abstract, like marriage? As it turns out, that's no exception. Everyone loves new relationships because there is so much promise and potential, and everything about the other person always seems so, well, new! In fact, most people decide to get married because they're convinced they'll feel the same way five, ten, and twenty years down the line as they do at the altar.

This makes sense because, when those potent feelings of love overwhelm you, it's easy to believe that the feeling will never go away. But what tends to get overlooked is that, after a certain period of time, that newness factor is going to diminish, and you will eventually adapt to your new circumstances. Instead of marriage being a constant whirlwind of love and passion like it was at the beginning of the relationship, it's also going to involve many mundane moments like entertaining in-laws and vegging out in front of the television together.

This is nothing to be discouraged about, because this happens in every marriage, but it's important to have a realistic understanding of what you can expect from adaptation before deciding to take the plunge. If you delude yourself into thinking that the ecstatic feeling you have at the beginning of a relationship will never change, it will inevitably lead to disappointment. Too often people think that something is wrong in a marriage because they don't feel the same as they did in the beginning, when passions were running at their highest. What they don't realize is that this is a completely normal occurrence in any relationship, and easily explainable by adaptation.

ADAPTING TO ADAPTATION

So what can you do about adaptation? Although you can't avoid it, you can mitigate its impact by acknowledging how it affects you. This means methodically thinking through all of the details and consequences of any significant decision you're contemplating, and doing your best to imagine how you will feel in the future as a result of that decision. If you are still okay with your decision after doing this exercise, then you'll be that much more confident that it's the right one, and the possibility of future regret will be diminished.

So before you rush into anything like buying an expensive material possession (is it really worth the extra money given the negligible impact on your long-term happiness?), getting a new tattoo (will you still love that dragon on your chest when you're 50?), or getting married (do you realize it's much more than wedding celebrations and a honeymoon?), do yourself a favor and take the time to consider how adaptation may affect you.

—————————————— LESSON ——————————————

Adaptation is a psychological phenomenon that helps explain why our initial excitement over something doesn't last forever. Taking the time to consider the potential effects of adaptation will help you avoid regrets such as buyer's remorse, and prepare you to make better life decisions about your future.

THERE WILL ALWAYS BE
SOMETHING TO WORRY ABOUT

*"How much pain they have cost us,
the evils which have never happened."*
—Thomas Jefferson

Does this scenario sound familiar? Something has happened in your life that you're worried about, and even though there's nothing you can do about it now, you find yourself paralyzed by this worry and unable to enjoy life in the same way. What's worse is that it's not just past events that have you worried; your anxiety also stems from negative future scenarios that haven't even happened yet, but that you've imagined in your mind.

You know from past experience that the things you worry about rarely turn out as bad as you fear, yet despite this, you still put your life on hold any time a new worry enters your mind. This is obviously not a healthy way to live, but what can you do about it? Worrying is something most people can't suppress or ignore, so trying to resist it is usually futile. The solution, instead, is to learn how to live your life *in spite* of worry.

DON'T DWELL ON
WHAT YOU CAN'T CONTROL

Whatever we worry about falls into one of two categories: the things we can do something about, and the things we can't. It's essential that you know the difference. If you're dealing with the first category, then the solution is obvious: take action and do something about it. For instance, if you're worried about something you've done wrong, taking action could mean acknowledging that you're at fault, sincerely apologizing, and making amends by whatever means necessary. If you're worried about losing your job, taking action could mean limiting expenses, learning new valuable skills, and looking for a new job. If you're worried about your health, taking action could mean improving your diet, exercising more, and getting regular check-ups.

> "Let our advance worrying become advance thinking and planning."
>
> —Winston Churchill

My brother, who tends to be a hypochondriac, always used to complain to me about how worried he was about his health. Until recently, he never made any effort to get in shape, was scared to see a doctor, and had what I'd generously describe as a poor diet. My response to him was always the same: unless you're going to make the minimal effort to act on what you can control regarding your health, you have no business complaining and *should be* worried!

The point is that we usually hold some degree of control when it comes to alleviating our worries, and when we do, we should always take appropriate action. It's when worries fall into the second category—the things we can't change—that we actually need to let go in order to move forward with life. Dwelling on what can't be changed results in an unnecessary struggle that causes both psychological and physiological harm.

Regardless of how much you'd prefer not to have any worries at all, learning to live with worry—not resisting it—should be your objective. The fact is, there will always be *something* to worry about, and it does no good to put your life on hold until all of your worries are resolved, especially when there is nothing more you can do about them. As foreign as it sounds, you can even allow yourself to be happy, in spite of any unresolved worries you have hanging over your head.

YOU CAN ENJOY LIFE IN SPITE OF WORRY

I've found myself plagued by worry too many times in life—over finding a job, problems with my health, even losing my hair. Despite acknowledging that I had done all I could to alleviate those concerns, I still wouldn't give myself permission to relax or be happy until each worry was fully resolved, even if that meant days, weeks, or months. By allowing something I couldn't change to affect my well-being, I lost interest in my work, my relationships suffered, and I just wasn't enjoying life. In truth, it would be very disheartening to know how many happy moments I've deprived myself of over the years on account of my incessant worrying. However, as my mom showed me on countless occasions, it *is* possible to move on and enjoy pockets of happiness, even in the face of the most debilitating worries.

In the late 1980s, my mom was first diagnosed with breast cancer. I was eleven at the time, and didn't have a good grasp of what cancer was or its potential ramifications. Instead, I was more preoccupied with what was going on in my own life such as school, Nintendo, and especially skiing. I loved skiing so much that when I learned about a weeklong ski trip to Canada being planned by some of my classmates, I begged my mom to take me. Seeing her children happy is what gave my mom immeasurable joy, and knowing how much I loved skiing, she readily agreed.

I was ecstatic when she told me, but lost in my excitement was the fact that she had already started weekly radiation therapy for her cancer. By going on this trip with me, it would mean she would miss at least a week of that treatment. Having cancer is something that would worry even the strongest of individuals, and deviating from the prescribed course of treatment would only add to that mental burden. My mom could have so easily stayed at home and continued with her treatment as planned, and no one would have faulted her. Instead, she courageously decided to double up on her radiation treatment one week, and then skip the following week, in order to take me skiing in Canada.

Despite harboring what must have been unimaginable worry, my mom refused to let it prevent her from enjoying a memorable week with her son. We wound up having an amazing time together that week, and not once did I see her unhappy or wallowing in self-pity. The bravery my mom demonstrated in this instance epitomizes what it means to enjoy life in spite of worry, and has inspired me beyond words.

IT'S OKAY TO WORRY, JUST NOT TOO MUCH

Life is way too short for constant worrying. As the years go by, the time spent worrying can accumulate into a significant portion of your life, without you even being aware of it. The question to ask yourself is: how much of your life are you willing to dedicate to worrying about things outside of your control, and how many happy moments, promising opportunities, and memorable experiences are you missing out on in the meantime by doing this? Without a doubt, events will occur during the course of your life that will worry you, and that's okay. You shouldn't resist those inevitable worries, but neither should you allow yourself to become stuck in place because of them.

LESSON

Life is too precious to be put on hold any time you're faced with a new worry, because there will always be *something* to worry about, and you can't always do something about it. Make it a goal to learn how to live your life in spite of worry, instead of struggling in vain to resist it.

FIX THE ROOT
OF THE PROBLEM

"The cause is hidden; the effect is visible to all."
—Ovid

All of us struggle with problems in life that we'd like to fix, whether it's a battle with weight gain, trust issues, or some other imperfection that prevents us from becoming our best selves. We do whatever we can to make the necessary self-improvements, but often wind up spinning our wheels as the same problems continue to manifest themselves over and over again.

There's a reason for this. When your efforts are only focused on treating the surface (or symptom) of a problem, a larger, more imbedded issue (the root) remains unaddressed, resulting in further symptoms and perpetual frustration. To use a simple analogy, think of a problem you face as an undesirable weed growing in your garden. If you're trying to get rid of that pesky weed by just cutting away the visible stem, it will soon grow back and nothing will have been solved. However, if you were to dig down deep and pull it out from the ground, root and all, then the weed (problem) will cease to exist.

THE ROOT OF A WEIGHT STRUGGLE

Battling weight gain can seem like a never-ending struggle where, despite strenuous effort, those extra pounds never seem to stay off for long. Anyone who has dealt with weight issues knows how frustrating this can be, but before reaching for diet pills or signing up for a quick-fix weight-loss program, focus instead on how you can attack the root of the problem. In addition to potential side effects, quick fixes are not at all sustainable, and the cycle of losing then gaining weight will continue indefinitely. At best, these shortcuts only address the surface issue (the fact that a person is overweight), not the root of the problem (what is *causing* the extra weight), so they offer no lasting solution.

With any weight issue, the root causes include factors that have not changed over time, such as the type of food we eat, our daily caloric intake, how much we exercise, and our genetic predisposition to weight gain. With the exception of the last one, all of these root factors can be fixed with proper effort and commitment. If we target the contributing factors leading to weight gain, weight loss will take care of itself.

I don't mean to make it sound like this is easily done, because anyone who has struggled with weight issues will tell you that it's a significant undertaking of modified eating habits, time-consuming exercise regimens, and overall lifestyle change. The point is that any effort you make should be aimed toward fixing the root of the problem, not just its symptoms.

JEALOUS MUCH?

I have been a jealous person for most of my life, particularly when it comes to relationships. I never acknowledged this about myself until after a number of failed relationships forced me to take a deeper look at what was causing them to fail. In the past, I would always try to fix my jealousy issues by replacing any girlfriend that I had deemed untrustworthy, falsely believing that *she* was causing me to act jealous. In fact, I used to naively believe that there had to be some magical girl out there who would never do anything to make me jealous, conveniently eliminating the need to confront the real cause of my problem.

I eventually figured out that the one consistent theme in my failed relationships was an inability to control my jealousy, so finding a new girlfriend would only offer a temporary fix to a deeper problem. If my jealous tendencies were the root cause of what was causing my relationships to fail, then they would play the same role in *all* of my future relationships. Once I accepted this, I started to work on fixing the root of the issue by learning how to control my jealous behavior.

Thankfully I was able to make significant progress in this area before meeting my wife, who has a very low tolerance for the kind of jealous outbursts I'd been prone to in my past. I am still by no means perfect, and I still struggle with jealousy issues at times, but I'm comforted by the fact that I was able to identify the root of my problem and take the necessary steps to address it.

LOOK BELOW THE SURFACE

If you ever find yourself struggling to fix the same problem over and over again to no avail, it's a safe bet there is something deeper, below the surface, that's not being addressed. In that case, you'll need to do two things: identify what is actually causing the problem to manifest itself, and then get to work on fixing it. How you go about fixing the root of any problem is up to you, but the point is that if you want to make *real* progress, any effort you make should be targeted at the root itself, and not just the symptoms on the surface.

——————————— LESSON———————————

Like constantly removing an unwanted weed that continues to resurface, treating the symptoms of any problem in life is never a permanent solution, and will only lead to frustration. The only real way to overcome a problem once and for all is to find, and then fix, the *root* of what's causing it.

HAPPINESS IS THE ULTIMATE CURRENCY

"Happiness should be the determinant of our actions,
the goal toward which all other goals lead."
—Tal Ben-Shahar, *Happier*

Every decision you make in life should be based on whether or not it will make you happy. No matter what other reasons you have for doing something, obtaining happiness should always be the ultimate motivation behind your decisions, because there is nothing beyond being happy.

No one says, "I want to be as happy as possible so that I can make a ton of money." That wouldn't make any sense, because it presupposes that having a ton of money would be better than being happy. Instead we believe (rightly or wrongly) that *if* we make a lot of money, *then* we will be happy. But it's vital that these kinds of assumptions are accurate, because there is little consolation in things like wealth, fame, and so forth if they are *not* going to make you happy. After all, what is the point of life if not to be as happy as possible?

PURSUING HAPPINESS
SHOULDN'T BE COMPLICATED

Many of us make obtaining happiness a lot more complicated than it should be. Whether it's adding unnecessary steps to reach happiness, or failing to prioritize the areas of our lives that make us most happy, we have a habit of trading the happiness that is right in front of us now, for the prospect of future happiness that isn't guaranteed.

Does the following sound familiar? "If I take this high-paying job (which I really won't like), work very hard (against my will), save enough money (after treating myself to certain comforts because of how stressful and depressing my job is), then I *should* (at some undetermined future point) be able to (enjoy life, have a comfortable retirement, take that trip, be happy)."

This type of long-winding path to happiness may eventually work out in the end, but why add *any* additional steps to get to the ultimate goal of happiness? The if-if-then mentality of needing prerequisite events in order to be happy denies us a great deal of happiness that could be accessible to us right now.

Not only that, but some of these links to happiness (job I hate › more money › happiness?) are based on faulty logic. Instead of making things harder on ourselves, we should always find the most direct, uncomplicated path to happiness. For instance, what if instead of choosing the job described above, you decided to take a less lucrative position more aligned with one of your passions? Although you may make less money, you would only be one step removed from happiness, which is really the currency you are after anyway (job I enjoy › happiness).

When I graduated from college in Chicago and began my first real job search, I remember feeling like it was one of the happiest periods of my life. At the time I had a girlfriend I was in love with, a group of friends I was very close to, and a future that seemed bright and promising. My ideal situation was to find a high-paying job in Chicago that would allow me to accumulate enough wealth to live the life I'd always imagined.

But as I went through the job application process, it began to dawn on me how difficult it would be to land the kind of high-paying job I was looking for in Chicago. There were plenty of such opportunities in New York City, but I was reluctant to move away since my girlfriend and friends, who lived locally, were a significant source of my current happiness. Eventually I was faced with a choice I didn't want to make: accept a high-paying job offer I received to work in New York, or stay in Chicago and look for a less lucrative job.

I was torn. If I stayed in Chicago, I'd remain close to my friends and girlfriend, but I wouldn't have that high-paying job I felt entitled to. If I accepted the position in New York, I'd be leaving my current source of happiness, but the money I'd be making *could* lead to *future* happiness. In the end I took the job in New York, having convinced myself I would only do it for a couple of years, make a lot of money, then move back to Chicago where everything would be waiting for me.

As you can probably guess, that was very naive thinking and (surprise!) things didn't work out like I had planned. I wound up spending five years in New York (not two), my girlfriend and I broke up after the first year, and I quickly lost touch with most of my close friends. As for the job, I did make good money, but I didn't enjoy what I was doing at all, and it was easily the most stressful period of my life.

When I look back on that experience, it's easy to see where I went so wrong. I added unnecessary steps to reach a happiness that I was already experiencing (move to NY › make a lot of money › move back to Chicago › be happy again), and I mistakenly thought more money would somehow justify the sacrifice of happiness provided by good friends and a girlfriend who loved me. It didn't.

CHOOSING THE OPTIMAL PATH TO YOUR HAPPINESS

As I learned the hard way, you should always choose the most direct, uncomplicated path to your happiness, because that's the ultimate currency you're seeking to begin with. If you're experiencing genuine happiness in your life right now, think long and hard before sacrificing that valuable currency for a future happiness that is in no way guaranteed.

It's also important to have sound assumptions about what's likely to provide you with the most happiness in life. Should pursuing happiness from something as ephemeral as wealth or fame take priority over what close friendships, romantic love, or life experience could offer you? Really take the time to analyze which areas of your life provide you with the greatest return of happiness, and then prioritize them accordingly. Remember, there's no standard path that you're obliged to take. The right path for *you* is the one that provides you with the most happiness.

Finally, choosing the optimal path to happiness requires considering whether the negative impact of your actions will outweigh the potential benefits. An easy way to think of this is that it's like maintaining a checking account, where you always want to end up with a positive balance after any transaction you make. In this case the transactions are the decisions you make in life, and your account balance is a measure of your net happiness. For example, would the happiness from pursuing your passion in art, music, or writing outweigh disappointing your parents who had other hopes for your career? Would the pleasure of sleeping with another person justify the guilt you'd experience from betraying your current partner? Would you be willing to trade the happiness of watching your kids grow up in order to earn more money and security for their future? When important questions like these are analyzed from the viewpoint of what will provide the greatest net happiness, it will lead to better life decisions.

Choosing to pursue what makes you most happy in life can take a great deal of courage and may result in others being disappointed by your actions. But again, what is the point of doing anything in life, if not to be happy?

HAPPINESS Q&A

Understandably, asserting that the fundamental point of life is to pursue happiness raises a number of questions. With that in mind, let me address a few of them here.

Isn't the point of life to serve others, not just to pursue our own happiness selfishly? I don't believe these two things are mutually exclusive. In fact, one of the best ways you can serve others is by being happy in their presence, and allowing your happiness to rub off on them. If doing things like volunteering your time, working for charitable causes, or helping the less fortunate brings you happiness, then by all means you should incorporate those activities into your life as much as possible. On the other hand, it won't do anyone much good if you're miserable trying to serve others out of guilt or obligation.

I make a lot of money at my job, but I enjoy it. Should I feel guilty about that? Absolutely not. Again, the point is to be happy, so if your job genuinely makes you happier, then all power to you. However, beyond a certain level, money is not going to provide additional happiness. So I would just caution you to keep a proper perspective, and ensure that nothing more fundamental to your happiness gets sacrificed as a result of accumulating wealth.

I can't just do whatever I feel like to pursue my own happiness. I have a family to support! You'd be doing your family a much better service by being happy yourself than by sacrificing your own happiness to ensure they have a life of privilege. The best example you can set for your spouse or kids is not spoiling them at the expense of your own happiness, and showing them that one can be happy despite not having all of the so-called luxuries of life.

When I first began to fly, it surprised me that the airlines advocated putting on your own oxygen mask before that of a small child. It didn't seem to make sense because I thought we should put the safety of our kids first before worrying about ourselves. Now it makes perfect sense to me. The safest thing you can do for your kids is to take care of yourself first so that they will be better served. It won't do them any good if you pass out while trying in vain to save, protect, or spoil them.

———— LESSON ————

Every decision in life should be based on whether or not it will bring you happiness. That is the ultimate currency we all seek, and no amount of money, pleasure, or sacrifice can ever make up for it or surpass it.

LIFE ISN'T FAIR

"Expecting the world to be fair to you because you are a good person is like expecting the bull not to charge because you are a vegetarian."
—Dennis Wholey

Life isn't fair, and sometimes bad things happen to good people. Real-life experience teaches us that we're not always rewarded for our good deeds, nor are we guaranteed a life free from hurt, injustice, or tragedy. Even if you follow all the rules, are well-behaved, and lead a sin-free life, it assures you nothing. Accepting this reality is a tough pill to swallow for many people, but naively believing otherwise inevitably leads to disappointment, bitterness, and sometimes even a loss of faith. Once you're able to let go of the notion that life somehow owes you something, or that it has to be fair, you'll quickly realize how important it is to live your best life *now*.

LIFE ISN'T AWARE THAT YOU'RE SPECIAL

If only life were predictable and fair, things would be so much easier. Wouldn't it be comforting to know that if you ate healthy and saw a doctor regularly that you'd never get sick, that if you were loyal and worked hard that you'd never be laid off, and that if you lived a sin-free life and did as you were told that you'd be shielded from hurt? Of course that would be great, but unfortunately things don't always work out that way.

In reality life is much more random than predictable, and nothing is ever guaranteed. As harsh as that sounds, our ability to accept this truth will go a long way in determining how we handle life's inevitable setbacks. For instance, if you insist that life should always be fair, and that all good behavior should be properly rewarded, then you'll undoubtedly feel resentment anytime life throws you a raw deal with the loss of a loved one, a career setback, or an unexpected illness. On the other hand, if you understand that nothing in life is assured, regardless of how great a person you may be, you'll view life's unexpected setbacks for what they really are: random and impersonal.

All of us would like to believe that we're "special" and immune to life's indifference to fairness. Not being an exception, I used to naively think that the maxim "life isn't fair" somehow didn't apply to people like me or my family. As far as I was concerned, we *were* special, and therefore entitled to a life free from suffering and injustice. Then one day I found out that my mom had a relapse of breast cancer, and it quickly dispelled any notion I had about life being fair. Although she had successfully defeated breast cancer twenty years prior, her cancer was now metastasized, stage four, and terminal.

To say that it was a travesty of justice for my mom to get cancer for a second time would be a colossal understatement. It just didn't seem fair that someone like my mom, who in every way was an extraordinary human being, had to deal with such an evil disease, particularly one that she had already defeated. I had an incredibly difficult time accepting the unfairness of it all, but ironically it was my mom, of all people, who had a calming influence on me. Despite the fact that she had sacrificed her whole life to make others happy, she knew that life didn't owe her anything in return, nor did it have to be fair. She was the victim of unfortunate circumstances and had every right to become bitter, but she never stopped being the incredibly kind, generous, and loving person that she had always been.

NOTHING IS ASSURED, SO LIVE THAT WAY

My mom's cancer, and eventual death, was a harsh way for me to learn that life doesn't have to be fair. But just like my mom, I refuse to let that awareness alter my way of life one bit. If anything, I'm now comforted by the fact that, regardless of whether or not life treats me fairly, I will still strive to do good, treat others well, and live every day to its fullest. And that's the point: rather than living your life based on the expectation that you'll be treated fairly, or that you're owed something in return for being a good person, live your life as if none of that is assured! This means living for the now, letting go of grudges, and doing things for the sake of themselves, instead of living in anticipation of some future reciprocation which is in no way guaranteed. You'll find that making this fundamental shift in perspective is surprisingly liberating, and frees you from the disappointment of life falling short of your expectations.

--- LESSON ---

We'd all like to believe that life is fair and just, and that none of our good deeds will go unrewarded, but unfortunately that's just not the case. The truth is that life can be random and unpredictable, and those expecting otherwise will only end up disappointed. However, accepting this reality does not have to be something negative. To the contrary, it should serve as an impetus to live your best life now, because *nothing* in life is ever guaranteed.

EFFORT COUNTS

*"Satisfaction lies in the effort, not in the attainment;
full effort is full victory."*
—Mahatma Gandhi

If you were to judge everything you did based solely on measurable external results, without consideration of the effort you put in, you'd experience a great deal of dissatisfaction in life. For better or worse, our society places an emphasis on quantifiable achievement—and less on effort, self-improvement, and learning for the sake of learning. The unspoken message we receive throughout school, athletics, and life in general is that effort is all well and good, but measurable results are what count.

This is not a fair way to judge yourself (or others), because not everything that is meaningful is measurable. So before beating yourself up for not coming in first place in that contest, or for not getting an A on that test, consider that there is plenty of satisfaction to be gained from giving your best personal effort in whatever you undertake.

A FAIRER WAY TO JUDGE

One consequence of placing too much emphasis on rewards, victories, and other external results is that you wind up being too hard on yourself. Most people don't give themselves enough credit for what can't be measured, such as effort and personal growth, and predicate too much of their self-worth on measurable, but less relevant, standards. Instead of taking pride in a job well done, or what we've learned in the process, we tend to judge ourselves based on whether we won or lost, what grade we got, or how high of a salary we were paid.

Don't get me wrong, I do believe it's important to have lofty standards to *strive toward,* but I don't believe our perception of ourselves should be based solely on attaining them. A fairer way to judge anything you do in life is to ask yourself the following question: *Did I do everything I could given my ability, resources, and knowledge at the time?* If the answer is yes, then there is nothing to regret, and you should feel proud of what you were able to learn and accomplish. If not, then at least you have room for improvement next time. At the end of the day, you're only human, and it won't do any good to chastise yourself if you truly did the best you could.

The same criterion applies to how we judge others. If we're critical of someone because they're not meeting some arbitrary standard that we've set for them, without appreciating the effort they're putting in, it's bound to create hard feelings. For example, insisting that your child improves her grades (or else!), or nagging your spouse to drop fifteen pounds, is not only insensitive but also ineffective.

These types of one-dimensional demands imply that you're not at all concerned with the effort someone is willing to make; you just want to see some external measurement improve. In turn, the other person perceives that, no matter how hard they try, it will never be good enough, leading to feelings of helplessness or rebellion. Instead of emphasizing the attainment of quantifiable goals as a gauge of someone's worth, it's more important to encourage the people you care about—a child, spouse, or whomever—to give their best effort at all times, and let the results take care of themselves. In fact, *all* relationships would be better served by learning to appreciate more than just what can be seen or measured.

WINNING ISN'T EVERYTHING,
OR THE ONLY THING

A good friend of mine is training to become a professional boxer and spends just about every waking moment of his life preparing to reach that goal. He eats a ridiculously healthy diet, doesn't drink or smoke, trains up to five hours a day, and is the most competitive person I have ever known. Every year he enters the state Golden Gloves tournament with hopes of qualifying for nationals and springboarding his professional career. One year he trained as hard as he's ever trained, was in the best shape of his life, and entered the tournament with a great deal of confidence. After winning his first round match, he lost a close decision in the semi-finals to a tough opponent, thus ending his dream of qualifying for nationals.

After the fight I was apprehensive about talking with him, presuming he'd be devastated with the result. To my surprise, he handled the defeat better than anyone could have expected. He said he was completely at peace with his personal effort, and left it all out in the ring. Of course he would have liked to win, but in no way could he get down on himself after giving it his all. I was completely thrown by this, because I had always thought that winning was the whole point of anything you do. Yet here was this intensely competitive friend of mine who, instead of being depressed by not achieving the victory he had worked so hard for, was proud of himself for his effort!

After that conversation, one thing immediately became clear to me: I had been way too hard on myself in my own life. I thought back to all those times I'd get depressed over things like not acing a test, losing a wrestling match, or failing to meet a goal, and never bothered to give myself credit for how well I prepared, the effort I gave, or what I learned in the process. Of course I would have liked to have received all A's, won all those matches, and achieved all those goals, but by only preoccupying myself with the external results, I essentially cheated myself out of the satisfaction that comes from self-improvement and giving something your all.

TAKE PRIDE IN YOUR EFFORT AND DEVELOPMENT

There are no awards handed out for those who give maximum effort or reach their full potential, yet those accomplishments mean more than any ranking or test score could ever indicate. To a certain extent, it's understandable why schools, businesses, and the like feel measurable standards are the most efficient way to determine someone's level of achievement, but that doesn't mean you should use those exact same standards to judge yourself.

No one has the innate talent, superior intellect, and graceful athleticism to finish first-place in everything they do. Instead of judging yourself harshly for not winning at something, or for not attaining every lofty goal you set, take pride in what you've learned, how much you've improved, and the knowledge that you applied yourself fully.

--------------------- LESSON ---------------------

People tend to judge themselves only by what they can see and measure. However, not everything that is meaningful is measurable, and you do yourself (and others) a huge disservice when personal effort is not given its due credit. There is plenty of satisfaction to be gained from doing your best in whatever you undertake, and you should be proud of what you learn, and how you grow, in the process.

AVOID SENSELESS ACTS AND ADDICTIONS

"It is easier to stay out than get out."
—Mark Twain

The world is filled with countless examples of senseless acts and addictions, such as smoking, doing drugs, and driving while intoxicated. These behaviors are some of the most avoidable causes of pain and suffering that we can inflict upon our health and that of others. The reasons for engaging in such activities, despite their well-known detrimental effects, include anything from a lack of knowledge, to peer pressure and inadequate planning. Fortunately, they can all be avoided.

CIGARETTES ARE KILLERS

What is the best way to prevent cancer, heart disease, stroke, emphysema, and an early death? Simple: don't smoke. Unless you have been living in a cave for the last few decades, anyone who smokes knows that cigarettes are

not just bad for you; they're horrible and can kill you. So by choosing to smoke, you're literally taking your life in your own hands. The scariest part is that it's easy to ignore this fact, since the most insidious damage takes place out of view in the heart, lungs, and blood. That is where debilitating diseases develop gradually and then strike without warning, usually when it's too late to do anything about it.

Tragically, your health is not the only thing at risk if you smoke. Secondary smoke is unquestionably harmful to others as well, whether it's at home or out in public, so using the excuse that you should just be left alone if you want to smoke is no longer justifiable. Unless you smoke all of your cigarettes in an airtight chamber, you are negatively affecting others with your habit.

Even the subtle consequences of smoking should not to be taken lightly. I know I am not alone when I say that I would have a difficult time dating someone who smokes. When you think about it, who'd want to kiss someone with smoky breath, smelly clothes, or nicotine-stained teeth? It's not attractive. Worse yet, smoking diminishes endurance, which hinders other aspects of intimacy!

The more you smoke, the more susceptible you become to the power of its addiction, so the best thing you can do is never start. Some people quit smoking for decades and still have moments when they crave a cigarette, which is indicative of just how strong nicotine addiction can be. One of the best things I ever did in my life was to give up smoking. I started when I was sixteen and didn't quit for over twelve years. Like most people who start smoking, I wanted to look cool and fit in, but all I was really doing was damaging my health and boyish good looks.

Not only that, but smoking significantly limited my potential as a competitive athlete, which is something I deeply regret to this day. What concerns me most, though, are the potential long-term health consequences that I'm not even aware of yet. The thought of having my life cut short because of foolishly smoking for all of those years truly scares me, and clearly, smoking was not worth it. So please do yourself, your health, and the health of others a favor, and don't smoke.

DRINKING AND DRIVING DON'T MIX

Drinking alcohol can be a pleasant, harmless experience when done safely and in moderation. However, there are a few major caveats: you need to be of legal age, you should never drink to the point where you are out of control, and you can never, *ever* get behind the wheel when you've been drinking.

Just for a second, try to picture this. You wake up from a hazy sleep feeling nauseous and with a splitting headache. For a few moments you're disoriented and don't know where you are. Then panic rushes over you when you start to recall fragments of memories from the night before: ambulance sirens, mangled cars, and your girlfriend's unmoving body in the passenger seat beside you. You try to convince yourself it was probably just a bad dream because nothing that terrible could ever happen to *you*. But that reprieve doesn't last long, and you realize it wasn't a dream; it really happened.

You look around, and to your horror recognize that you're lying on the floor of a jail cell with other not-so-friendly looking inmates staring at you. Reality hits you like a sledgehammer, and your heart sinks into the pit of your stomach. A million questions race through your mind: "How did this happen?" "Do my parents know where I am?" "Is my girlfriend injured?" Without knowing the answers to these questions, you have a sickening feeling that your life will never be the same. As you feel your world shattering around you, one last unavoidable question passes through your mind: "How could I have been so stupid to drink and drive?"

All it takes is one bad decision for your life to be ruined forever. Aside from putting your own physical well-being in harm's way, drunk driving accidents can result in a lifetime of pain and suffering for everyone affected by your actions, which is not something you'd ever want to bear on your conscience. And it's not just the people directly involved in the accident that you'd be harming, either. It's all the friends, relatives, and loved ones who would suffer as well—all as a result of one poor decision.

Even if you're fortunate enough to avoid an accident while driving under the influence, a DUI arrest is no picnic either. At a minimum you're looking at a night in jail, an impounded car, thousands of dollars in legal fees, a suspended license, and numerous other hassles that you will not enjoy dealing with. And all of that is considered getting off easy for a first offense. One of my friends got a DUI (his first) a few years ago for just barely being over the legal limit. The time it took him to go through the whole court process, pay all of the fines, get his car back, and have his license reinstated, was around two years. *Two years* of hassle and significant financial loss, all because of a split-second, seemingly innocuous decision to get behind the wheel after drinking a little too much.

Just like properly preparing to have safe sex, you have to plan ahead when you know there's a chance you'll be out drinking, because all your knowledge about doing the right thing in these situations becomes useless once you've had too much to drink and can't think clearly. After a few drinks out at a party or bar, you may convince yourself that you're fine to drive home, even though you're not. (Remember: you don't have to feel drunk for your driving ability to be impaired, or for you to be over the legal limit. Don't find out the hard way.)

In order to avoid any such irrational decisions, you have to take action beforehand by designating a driver, or arranging a ride. Once you take care of these details with a rational and sober state of mind, you can relax and enjoy yourself without worrying about making a regrettable decision later on. Even if you wind up in a situation where you've had a few drinks unexpectedly, take a cab home and have a friend (or another cab) bring you back to your car the next day. This is something I have done on a number of occasions, and it has undoubtedly kept me out of trouble. If you think about it, what's worse? Spending a few extra dollars and dealing with a few minutes of inconvenience? Or putting yourself at risk of unspeakable consequences that could last a lifetime?

DOING DRUGS IS A LOSING PROPOSITION

People take recreational drugs for a variety of reasons, such as peer pressure, an escape from pain, or an attempt to generate more excitement than what real life provides. But regardless of one's motivation for doing drugs, quite simply it's a losing proposition. Trust me when I tell you that there is not a single drug in existence that leaves you feeling better off than where you started. Add to that the risk of overdosing, the pain it causes people who care about you, and the significant long-term negative health effects on the mind and body, and the obvious question becomes: Why do drugs in the first place?

Here's a useful analogy: In any business, approval for a new project is usually granted or declined based on whether it's expected to generate a positive *net present value* (NPV). A positive NPV means that the project will, in the short- or long-run, generate a profit. The CEO of any business will never give approval for a project that is expected to generate a negative NPV, because they don't want their company to lose money and wind up worse off than where it started.

It should be no different for you when considering drugs. As CEO of your own company (your body and overall health), it's senseless to do something that will knowingly make you worse off than you were before you started.

You never get something for nothing, and there is always a cost. When you do drugs and experience *unnatural* highs, your brain will build up a tolerance to the pleasure-inducing chemicals that you need in order to feel good, setting a lofty bar for your happiness that becomes progressively harder to achieve from everyday life experience.

I have witnessed this phenomenon firsthand with a number of people close to me who have done drugs. Most of them have thankfully moved on from their habit, but the lingering effects are still evident. The worst part is that they could have everything going for them—a loving family, great job, and plenty of security—but they always talk as if their best days are behind them. Listening to them talk you get the sense that, no matter how great their current reality is, past drug use has undermined their ability to appreciate it. This is depressing, because obtaining real happiness in life is difficult enough as it is. Why make it harder on yourself?

The best way to avoid the detrimental consequences of drugs is to never start in the first place. If you never start, you'll never think you're missing out on some unobtainable high that will undermine your present reality. If you do start, the consequences of addiction will grow more severe the longer you keep it up. Not surprisingly, you never hear someone say they used cocaine for twenty years and then just gave it up on a whim without any problems. You never hear that because it's never that easy. Significant psychological and physiological addiction is formed in the process of continual drug abuse, and requires a lot more than just a change of heart to overcome.

If you've done drugs or have contemplated doing them, it's important to realize there are things in everyday life that generate an equal, if not greater, feeling than any drug could provide. These are activities that offer *natural* highs. With natural highs, it's possible to experience ecstasy-like feelings in your life, without the crutch of drugs. Here are some examples:

- Runner's high: Occurs after a certain amount of physical exertion. When you experience this, your brain naturally secretes endorphins such as dopamine that give you mental clarity and an incredible natural high.

- Overcoming fears: Can be anything you're afraid of but do anyway, such as approaching someone you're interested in, speaking in public, or even skydiving. Usually comes in the form of an adrenaline rush.

- Good music: Dancing or even just listening to music can be hypnotic and put you into a state of natural ecstasy.

- Doing something you love: Engaging in anything you have a passion for or consider a hobby. People doing something they are passionate about report getting into a "zone," where time seems to stop and you simply cruise on an abundance of natural good feelings.

- Having something to look forward to: Things like planning a vacation, a special night with someone you care about, or even just time for yourself, can all provide pleasant feelings of anticipation and motivation.

- **Doing something nice for someone:** Requires such little effort, but provides a tremendous benefit for yourself, as well as for those you help. A great deal for everyone!

- **Sex:** Self-explanatory! This natural high is exponentially more intense when done with someone you're in love with, and should always be done safely.

- **Reaching your potential:** This can mean a variety of things, such as achieving something you've worked hard for, or evolving as a person.

- **Meditation:** Closing your eyes and letting your mind settle into its least excited state brings about an experience of pleasure and pure bliss.

--- LESSON ---

Smoking, driving while intoxicated, and doing drugs are all examples of behaviors that are hazardous to your health and the health of others. They are also *completely avoidable*. It's incumbent upon you to resist engaging in these behaviors at any cost or inconvenience, because life is too precious to be cut short or marred by senseless acts and addictions.

DON'T TAKE THINGS PERSONALLY

"When you are immune to the opinions and actions of others,
you won't be the victim of needless suffering."
—Don Miguel Ruiz

Not everyone is going to like you. Accept that, because it's a fact of life. It's nothing personal; it's just that some people have quirky tastes and may be unimpressed by your best qualities. Even if you were to look like Brad Pitt, act like Mother Teresa, and have the wealth of Bill Gates, there would still be people out there who aren't too keen on you. With that in mind, my question to you is: *so what?* What does it really matter what someone else thinks of you, and why should it affect what you think of yourself or how you live your life? It shouldn't, because you know yourself better than anyone else does, and ultimately it's *your* opinion of yourself that matters most.

A THICK SKIN HAS ITS BENEFITS

I've been rejected so many times that, if I took it all personally, I would never have accomplished anything in my life. I've been rejected by so many girls I've lost count. Just about every college that I applied to rejected me. When I interviewed for jobs after college, I was rejected by every company I met with except one. The only reason I was still able to get into the school that I wanted, find a job that suited me, and marry the kind of girl I was seeking was because I never took the prior rejections personally, and I never stopped believing in myself. What I learned from those experiences is that you can't control whether or not you'll be liked or accepted, but what you can control is how you let it affect you.

Oftentimes the reason you won't be accepted for something (or by someone) is simply due to bad timing, and may have nothing to do with *you* at all. If you act spitefully toward someone because you're hurt or embarrassed by their rejection, then you'll immediately disqualify yourself from any further opportunities with that person, company, etc. That's why it's important not to let rejection affect you or your behavior, especially when it's due to factors outside of your control.

For example, let's say you've applied for a job that you really desire. You had a few interviews, made it through a few rounds, and then got passed over because the company didn't think you were the right fit at the time. Now, there are a few ways you could go from here. You could yell at the person interviewing you, swearing they'll regret this decision for the rest of their life (not recommended). You could walk away with your head down, thinking to yourself: "I knew they'd reject me." Or ideally, instead of being bitter or despondent, you could take it in stride by asking the company what you could do to improve your candidacy, and that you'd like to maintain contact in case another opportunity should arise.

If this is really a job you want, why not do everything in your power to show them that, despite being turned down (for now), you're willing to do whatever it takes to change their minds? I have seen this happen on countless occasions; someone is initially passed up by a college, job, lover, or whatever, only to be given another opportunity later on when the timing was more appropriate. People always seem to remember that person who impressed them with their ability to handle rejection with class and show persistence. It makes them want to find an excuse to give the person another shot, or even help find them something that's a better fit. It goes without saying that these kinds of second chances don't occur when you burn bridges out of spite, or when you just fade into the background without so much as a peep.

CONSIDER THE MESSENGER

There will be times in your life where there's a very clear divide between what someone thinks of you and what you think of yourself. But no one knows you better than you do. So before taking anything personally, always consider who is doing the judging, and whether their criticism has merit.

I was a terrible student throughout most of high school, and was very close to missing out on my dream of enrolling at a top-notch university. The low point came when my physics teacher, apparently underwhelmed by my D average, told me in no uncertain terms that I wouldn't amount to anything, and that I certainly had no business being in her class.

At first I let what she said really get to me, and I began to wonder whether she might be right. But then it dawned on me that this teacher hardly knew me, and she certainly had no way of getting inside my head to know what I was capable of, or how motivated I could be, when I applied myself.

When I look back on that situation now, I realize I was at an important crossroads in my life. If I continued to take personally what my teacher had said, then her prophecy would have likely turned out to be accurate. On the other hand, if I trusted *my own* beliefs about myself and what I was capable of, then I'd turn out fine. Thankfully, I chose the latter route. Instead of being distraught over what this teacher mistakenly thought of me, I tapped into the potential I always believed I had in order to turn my grades around and get into a great university.

SOME CRITICISM CAN BE CONSTRUCTIVE

Lastly, I do believe there are things that you should take, if not personally, at least into consideration. For instance, if someone you're close to, and whose opinion you trust, tactfully suggests a few things you can do to improve yourself, at a minimum it's worth listening to. You may not agree with everything they tell you, and ultimately it's what you believe about yourself that should still matter most. However, there's certainly no harm in being receptive to constructive criticism from those who know you best, particularly if it helps you develop into a better human being.

———————————— LESSON————————————

No one knows yourself better than you do. Instead of taking any outside criticism or rejection too personally, keep focused on what you believe about yourself and what you're capable of, and always consider who is doing the judging.

TRUST YOUR INSTINCTS

"We each need to let our intuition guide us, and then be willing to follow that guidance directly and fearlessly."

—Shakti Gawain

Have you ever had a gut feeling about something, ignored it, then later discovered it was trying to tell you something important? I have made this mistake on countless occasions, mostly because my instincts told me something I didn't want to hear. What I've come to learn is that if we trust these instincts, despite how harsh they seem, we'll find they are only looking out for our best interest. Instincts pick up on things we are not consciously aware of, and provide real guidance on all aspects of life from relationships to career choices—if only we'll listen.

That's what instincts do, and that's why we should trust them. When we ignore certain instincts because we're afraid of what they're trying to tell us, we're likely to choose a course of action that can have detrimental results.

IGNORANCE ISN'T BLISS

Relationships are a fitting place to start when it comes to learning how to trust your instincts. For instance, whenever we first start dating someone and things are going well, it's easy to conjure up the belief that *this could be the one!* Since we want to believe that this relationship is everything we have hoped for, we are likely to ignore anything that would tarnish the image we have of our new special someone. But there may come a moment in the relationship where that person does or says something that raises a clear red flag in our minds. It may even start out as something relatively innocuous—a mistruth, condescending comment, or jealous tendency— but it's enough to get our attention.

We can conveniently ignore these instincts because we don't like what they signify (our special someone isn't so special after all), but willful ignorance won't change the facts. The truth is we experience instincts like this *for a reason*. By ignoring them, we are setting ourselves up for future pain and distress that could easily have been avoided.

One particular instance of this stands out in my mind about a girl I used to date, whom I'll call Lisa. In the beginning, everything with Lisa was as perfect as could be. We spent nearly all of our free time together, got along splendidly, and were falling in love with each other. I was convinced beyond a shadow of a doubt that she was really *the one*.

Then she became dishonest with me, for no apparent reason and with no apologetic explanation. It started out as innocent white lies, and soon escalated to blatant deceptions. I knew in my gut this was a very bad sign, but I somehow managed to suppress my instincts and continued with the relationship (the charade, really). Despite the warning my instincts were sending me, I simply wasn't ready to face the truth that my "perfect" relationship was crumbling and that I was actually dating someone untrustworthy.

Not surprisingly, the lies and red flags continued to accumulate until I finally worked up the courage to confront her. She denied everything, of course, but at that point it didn't make a difference. In reality the relationship had been over for quite some time, and my self-respect was at an all-time low. Had I acted sooner, I would have spared myself a lot of unnecessary pain. I told myself over and over again that I should have known she was untrustworthy, that the warning signs were all there. But I did know! I just chose to ignore my instincts.

> "Good instincts usually tell you what to do long before your head has figured it out."
>
> —Michael Burke

Although it's important to trust your instincts in relationships, it's equally important not to do anything too hasty or rush to judgment. In fact, any red flag your instincts pick up on may just be a one-time thing that is easily explainable and resolvable. Regardless, if it has the potential to affect your relationship, then it's in your best interest to address the other person about it at the time the incident occurs. If that doesn't solve the problem, and the red flags continue to manifest themselves, then trust that your instincts are warning you about looming trouble and have the courage to walk away.

LET YOUR GUT GUIDE YOU

Your instincts serve a much greater purpose than just helping you avoid potential heartache. As you become more familiar with the signals to look for, they can also lead you toward positive ends. For example, your instincts can help guide you toward a career that captivates you, and may even help you discover a passion for something you never even considered previously.

This happened to me a number of years ago when I interviewed for a job with an investment company. Investing as a career was not something I ever had given thought to, let alone something I had experience in, but I needed a job and this was available. As part of the investment company's evaluation process (and much to my dismay), I was asked to complete a time-consuming project that would gauge my ability to analyze potential investments. Making matters worse, I was given only two days to do it and would have to work through the weekend.

As much as I expected to hate the assignment, I was surprised to find I actually enjoyed it. In fact, I found myself enthralled by the project and everything related to investing. I knew then and there that investing was a field I had a natural passion for and could be successful at. Prior to doing that project, I had no idea that investing was something I even remotely liked, but I couldn't deny what my instincts were telling me. What I discovered is that it really doesn't matter what the activity is, or how you *think* you'll feel about it. If doing it keeps you engaged, motivated, and excited, then you have just stumbled upon a new passion—a passion you can turn into a successful career.

Along similar lines, it's not unusual to have instincts about an ingenious idea, theory, or invention that could help improve people's lives or the world at large. Whenever we have such inspirations, it's common to believe that, if it was such a good idea, then someone else probably thought of it, tested it, and failed with it already; otherwise it would be well-known and accepted.

By dismissing our instincts out of hand like this, we could be denying ourselves and others the benefit of our genius. The truth is, everything hasn't been discovered already. In fact, some of the most life-altering ideas (gravity, evolution, Netflix) weren't discovered for a long time, in spite of how evident they became once someone pointed them out. So the next time you have a flash of ingenuity about *anything,* go with your gut and pursue it further. As a wise man once said, "Discovery consists of seeing what everybody has seen and thinking what nobody has thought." [5]

DECIPHERING YOUR INSTINCTS

It's important to acknowledge *any* instinct (hunch, premonition, intuition) once you become aware of it, then contemplate why you experienced it at that given time. What significance does it have? What is it trying to tell you? More often than not, an instinct will be coupled with an emotion that helps you decipher the message.

For instance, if the coupled emotion is *excitement,* maybe your instincts are trying to give you an insight into something you should pursue further

---

5 Albert Szent-Gyorgyi, *Irving Good, The Scientist Speculates*

like an idea, passion, or career that will captivate you. If the coupled emotion is *uneasiness,* maybe your instincts are saying something has occurred that doesn't sit well with you and that you should make an effort to resolve it. If the emotion is *nervousness,* like butterflies in your stomach, maybe your instincts are suggesting you have an opportunity to grow in some way by overcoming a fear.

Regardless of the instinct, the process is always the same: recognize, contemplate, act. With enough practice and experience, you'll soon be able to recognize even the most subtle intuition, understand the significance of what it's telling you, and feel confident it is guiding you toward a course of action that serves your best interest. Take it from Richard Branson, Chairman of Virgin Group and entrepreneur extraordinaire, who used his gut instincts to create some of the world's most innovative companies, making himself a billionaire in the process:

> "Your instincts and emotions are there to help you. They are there to make things easier. For me, business is a 'gut feeling,' and if it ever ceased to be so, I think I would give it up tomorrow. By 'gut feeling,' I mean that I believe I've developed a natural aptitude, tempered by huge amounts of experience, that tends to point me in the right direction rather than the wrong one. As a result, it also gives me the confidence to make better decisions."[6]

--- LESSON ---

You have instincts for a reason, and learning to trust them will help guide you toward better life decisions. At times instincts may not tell you what you want to hear, and may urge you to take action outside of your comfort zone, but ultimately they exist to serve your best interest.

---

6 Richard Branson, *Business Stripped Bare*

PEORLE RARELY CHANGE

"When we are no longer able to change a situation,
we are challenged to change ourselves."
—Viktor Frankl, *Man's Search for Meaning*

Everyone, at some point in their lives, has experienced the frustration of seeing someone's ability to change fall way short of expectations. Promises such as "from now on I will be different," or "this is the last time I will do that," ring hollow as that person's same old predictable characteristics manifest again and again.

Despite our logical reasoning and cogent arguments to make others see the error of their ways, our influence in changing someone's behavior has less of an effect than we might think. In fact, it's somewhat arrogant on our part to assume we have the power to change the way someone is, and it's *very* arrogant to assume someone should change for our benefit. This statement is not meant to be discouraging, but rather a reality check for what we can expect from someone we are desperately hoping will conform to our wishes.

TALK TO ME IN A YEAR

Despite our best intentions to help someone we care about change for the better, the ultimate responsibility lies with that person, and change is not easily accomplished. No one changes overnight from being untrustworthy to trustworthy, jealous to not jealous, insecure to confident, or irresponsible to responsible. Significant changes like these take time to develop, and don't result from good advice, talking about it, or promising to be different.

On the contrary, changing part of your fundamental character requires strong voluntary will, discipline, and (most importantly) repetitive real-world practice. Anything short of that is just wishful thinking and unlikely to have a lasting impact.

A friend of mine has a great response for anyone who swears to him they are going to change something meaningful about themselves: "Talk to me in a year." I love that response, because it's a simple, yet appropriate, challenge. Anyone can promise anything about how they are going to change. However, after a year's time it will become clear if that person has had the will and discipline to see the promised change through, and can then be taken seriously. A good rule of thumb to remember is that past action (not what someone has said or promised) is the best predictor of future behavior.

My parents got divorced when I was too young to remember. I was raised by my mom, but my dad lived close by, and I saw him often. I've always had a very stable relationship with my dad. He never hit me, always provided financial support when necessary, and was very reliable for that airport pickup. However, I can't say he provided the same type of love that my mom did. When I was younger, this used to bother me quite a bit. I just couldn't understand why my dad was not as interested or involved in my life as my mom was. I naively thought that emotional outbursts and heart-to-heart talks would get him to change, but nothing worked.

It took me a good number of years to realize that my dad is just the way he is, and that's not likely to change. The way I saw it, I could either continue to be frustrated by his inability to meet my expectations, or I could just accept him for the way he is. One thing was certain, I wasn't going to cut him out of my life just because he didn't live up to the ideals that I had for him as a father. But what I could do (and did) was adjust my expectations, and that has made all the difference in our relationship.

I can honestly say that I love and appreciate my dad, and I don't mean to single him out here because there have been others—family members, friends, girlfriends—whom I have felt equally frustrated by on account of their inability to change. Yet despite those frustrations, it's now clear to me that the problem was not so much them, but rather my unrealistic expectations.

CHANGE YOU CAN BELIEVE IN

It's certainly not impossible for people to make significant changes in themselves. I have witnessed many insecure people evolve into secure people, introverted people change to outgoing, and mean people become kind. However, in every one of these instances, the person was very committed and motivated to see that change through, no matter the effort or how long it took. So if you ever find yourself hoping that someone you care about is going to change for the better, the question you should answer honestly is if that person is dedicated, disciplined, and motivated enough to accomplish the change.

If the answer is "not likely," then what's the solution? If someone's inability to change is leading to a never-ending cycle of frustration and disappointment, but you'd still like to have them in your life, there is only one thing left to do: *change your expectations*. Ultimately, the frustration you are feeling is due to unmet expectations that you have created in your mind about how someone should behave. If you can accept the fact that people rarely change, and manage your expectations accordingly, it will weaken the ability of others' actions (or inactions) to negatively affect your well-being.

Empathy helps a great deal as well. I'm sure if we all examined our own lives, we'd realize it's equally hard for us to make significant fundamental changes in ourselves. That humble knowledge should go a long way in helping us understand what the other person is up against, and remind us to be more sympathetic when change doesn't happen the way we had hoped.

> "Consider how hard it is to change yourself and you'll understand what little chance you have in trying to change others."
>
> —Jacob M. Braude

—————————————— LESSON ——————————————

If you think everyone you know and care about is eventually going to change for *your* benefit, or conform to what *you* think is appropriate behavior, then you'll be constantly disappointed in life. Contentment doesn't arrive externally from other people conforming to what you wish. It's only derived from within, through our acceptance of others for who they are.

DON'T TAKE GOOD FRIENDS
FOR GRANTED

*"True friendship is like sound health; the value of it
is seldom known until it is lost."*
—Charles Caleb Colton

I t's surprising how easy it is to take good friends for granted. Despite the unquestionable value they add to our lives, good friends often get the short end of the stick when it comes to our best efforts and highest priorities—made obvious anytime we act disingenuous, abandon them for a new love interest, or fail to stay in contact. If we're lucky, our friends will take us back with open arms despite these flaws, because that's what friends are for.

However, everything works both ways. If we continually take our good friends for granted, we'll eventually become less of a priority for them as well. This should matter, because close friendships form an indispensable component of our overall happiness.

TO HAVE GOOD FRIENDS,
BE A GOOD FRIEND

Not taking good friends for granted starts with being trustworthy. Maintaining trust with anyone is important, but if that person is someone you consider a good friend, then it's essential. Close friends put a great deal of trust in each other, and are liable to suffer greatly if that trust is ever broken in some way. If we're ever lied to, let down, or taken advantage of by someone we presume to be our close friend, it can feel like a dagger has been thrust straight through our heart, and kills any chance of trusting that person in the same way again.

That's why it's imperative to be trustworthy with your close friends at all times, because if *they* can't trust you, then who can? In order to be considered trustworthy, you need to give friends the confidence that when they ask you for an important favor, you'll try your best to take care of it; that when they share something with you in confidence, you'll respect their wishes and not reveal it to anyone; that when they ask for your honest opinion, you'll give it to them straight without sugarcoating.

The same can be said of being open and genuine with good friends. It's completely natural to want the respect and approval of those we are closest too, even if that means embellishing stories about ourselves and shading out any negative details that might cast us in an unflattering light. I've certainly been guilty of this on occasion. Anytime something embarrassing ever happened to me, or whenever I had a problem I was ashamed of, I would just usually keep it to myself. Even when I hung out with my closest friends, I would resist discussing certain personal things out of fear that revealing them would make me look weak or lead to ridicule.

Then it dawned on me one day: If I couldn't even be genuine with my closest friends, I wasn't really all that genuine. So from that day forward I decided I would be more open about myself, and not keep everything so guarded as I had done in the past. Instead of feeling weak or ridiculed as I had feared, making this change actually took a huge weight off my chest, and allowed my friends to provide me with much-needed advice. In fact, opening myself up more encouraged my friends to be more open with me, making our relationships that much stronger.

In order to cultivate meaningful friendships, we should all drop our social masks and have the courage to confide in one another, because there is something truly special about sharing your greatest fears, wildest dreams, and most embarrassing stories with a good friend.

> "What happens when one person takes the risk to say to another: I'm confused, I'm not sure where I'm going; I'm feeling lost and lonely; I'm tired and frightened. Will you help me? The effect of such vulnerability is almost invariably disarming. 'I'm lonely and tired too,' others are likely to say and open their arms to us.
>
> But what happens when we try to maintain a 'macho' image of having it all together, of being the top dog, when we gird ourselves about with our psychological defenses? We become unapproachable, and our neighbors guard themselves in their defenses, and our human relationships become no more meaningful or productive than two empty tanks bumping against each other in the night."
>
> —M. Scott Peck, *What Return Can I Make?*

PRIDE AND OTHER FRIENDSHIP KILLERS

One of the main reasons friends fail to stay in touch can be summed up in a single word: pride. Pride is the reason we ask ourselves why *we* should make the effort to keep in touch with someone, when that person could just as easily make the same effort to get in touch with us. Sadly, the problem with this kind of stubbornness is that neither person winds up contacting the other, and as more time goes by, the more likely it is to stay that way.

This is obviously not a desired outcome if having that particular friend in your life is valuable to you. So the real question to ask yourself is: *Do I value this friendship enough to put my pride aside and make an effort to reach out to this person?* If you're honest with yourself, the answer will be clear.

Another mistake many people make is investing all their time and energy in a romantic relationship at the expense of their good friends. Quite often these friends have a long track record of being dependable and supportive, whereas the new love interest does not. The irony is that, if the love relationship turns sour, those same friends are the first ones they'll run to for comfort, pleading how us guys or girls have to stick together (until of course the next love interest comes along).

Reaching out to your friends only when you need something is a very unambiguous way of revealing how much you take them for granted. Your friends may welcome you back with open arms when this happens the first, second, or even third time, but they'll eventually get the hint that you only see them as a means to an end.

I can't tell you how many times I've witnessed someone invest everything in their romantic relationship at the expense of their friends, only to lose both in the end. It's almost a no-win situation because, even if the love interest does work out, the lover will not (and should not) replace the happiness that good friends provide. So no matter how in love you may think you are with someone, never be entirely dependent on them for your happiness, *especially* when it comes at the expense of your good friends.

NOT ALL FRIENDS ARE CREATED EQUAL

There is a real distinction between good friends and acquaintances, and not all friends are created equal. In fact, it isn't necessarily the *quantity* of friends that matters so much, but rather the *quality* of relationships that you're able to develop. I have several friends and acquaintances who don't get nearly the same priority that my few good friends get, and I am completely fine with that. It's much more rewarding to develop deep bonds with those select friends—getting to know them, building trust, and sharing experiences—than it is to spread myself over a large number of acquaintances where I can't possibly invest the same effort.

I'm also aware that any future decision to move away from my good friends would be a difficult one, and one I hope to never have to make. I consider myself extremely fortunate to live only a few blocks away from a number of close friends, and the happiness I receive from the time we're able to spend together is priceless. Giving that happiness up in exchange for a higher-paying job, warmer weather, or a new life elsewhere, is something I'd be very reluctant to do, and nothing I would ever do lightly.

GOOD FRIENDSHIP IS IRREPLACEABLE

There is nothing in life that could ever, nor should ever, make up for good friendship. Even if you have everything else going for you—a great marriage, an abundance of wealth, five-hundred Facebook friends—if you're lacking genuine friendship, you'll notice the difference. Good friends are hard to find, and even harder to replace, so never take them for granted.

—————————————— LESSON ——————————————

Good friendships form an essential component of our overall happiness. Instead of taking those select, invaluable relationships for granted, make every effort necessary to nourish and strengthen them. This means acting like a good friend yourself by being genuine, trustworthy, and committed to making close friends a continual high priority in your life.

GIVE THANKS

"The deepest principle in human nature is the craving to be appreciated."
—William James

When someone goes out of their way to do something nice for you, it's important to let them know it's fully appreciated. Even if your gratitude is delivered in the form of a simple and sincere "thank you," expressing your gratitude is always appropriate. Despite the claims of some people that they don't do things expecting to be thanked, *everyone* likes knowing that what they do for others is valued—whether that person is a parent, friend, lover, or even random stranger.

SINCERE GRATITUDE IS REINFORCING

Expressing your appreciation to someone who has done something nice for you is not only appropriate, but also serves as a form of positive reinforcement. By letting someone know that what they've done has not gone unnoticed, and that you're very grateful, you'll be giving that person significant motivation to repeat that behavior in the future. It's amazing how hard someone will strive to conform to the positive image we have of them, especially if that image is reinforced properly.

For example, let's say your girlfriend or boyfriend goes out of their way to cook you a special dinner. They spend their day buying ingredients, setting the table, and preparing a delicious meal just the way you like it. If you *sincerely* tell that person how much you appreciate the effort they put into that dinner, and that they've made you the happiest person in the world at that moment, they'll be highly motivated to cook more delicious dinners for you in the future. It will register that they've done something that makes you happy, thereby creating a strong connection between their actions and your reaction.

For some people (especially men), the problem with expressing gratitude is that they feel awkward vocalizing their feelings, or feel that it's a form of weakness to acknowledge that they needed the help of others. If it doesn't come naturally to express your appreciation verbally, then express it in your own way by buying that person lunch, sending flowers, or just giving them a hug. Silent gratitude doesn't do anyone much good, and withholding your appreciation from someone is not worth saving your pride over. If someone feels that what they do for another person goes unappreciated, sooner or later that lack of positive reinforcement will discourage their helpful behavior.

Saying thanks should not be overdone either. Of course it's important to show your appreciation when appropriate, but if you find yourself saying "thank you" mechanically five or ten times in a conversation, your expressions of appreciation will become diluted and lose their effect. Finally, don't even bother expressing your gratitude if you don't mean it. Most people can detect insincerity from a mile away, so you're better off not saying anything at all.

MAKE IT PERSONAL

There are a variety of ways to express gratitude, but the ones that have the greatest impact are those done with a personal touch. Examples may include a phone call, a small gift, or even looking someone directly in the eye and saying: "Thank you for ... (fill in the blank)."

My personal favorite is mailing a handwritten letter. With the advent of technology—email, texts, instant messaging—the use of personal communication like handwritten letters has become somewhat of a lost art. Try to remember how nice it feels to receive a love letter, thank you note, or birthday card (with money in it!), and that's the exact same feeling you'll be providing to someone who deserves it. Sending an email or text is better than doing nothing at all, but it's still somewhat impersonal. In contrast, mailing a handwritten letter or card communicates that you're willing to make the effort to express your appreciation in a personal way.

Expressing thanks at random times also works extremely well and doesn't have to be for something specific. In fact, an unplanned demonstration of gratitude has a much greater impact than when someone *expects* to be thanked. For instance, I guarantee that if you choose a random day to send your mom or girlfriend a dozen roses with an attached note that says, "I just wanted to let you know how much I appreciate the way you are and everything you do for me," they'll be completely surprised and overjoyed. Sending flowers on Valentine's Day or Mother's Day is nice, but to a certain degree it's expected, so the impact is not quite the same.

A SMALL BIT OF GRATITUDE GOES A LONG WAY

When I was in my first year of work after college, I was rather insecure about how I was performing at my job, and even contemplated quitting on a number of occasions. At one point during the year, I got involved with a relatively significant transaction for our firm, and after many months of stress, client meetings, and late-night work sessions, the deal finally wrapped up. I knew I had worked extremely hard on that deal, but it was thankless work, and I wasn't even sure if I had done a decent job.

To my complete surprise, I received a thank-you note from my boss soon thereafter. The small handwritten note complimented me on the quality of my work and expressed sincere gratitude for my effort over the previous months. That small display of appreciation instantly eliminated any doubts I had about my job performance, and from that day forward I was highly motivated to conform to the positive image my boss had of me.

Still to this day, I cite that note as the main reason why my confidence and motivation turned around at work. But beyond that, it made me realize how powerful of an impact expressing sincere appreciation can have on another person, even if it's in the form of a simple note. So no matter what method you choose to express your appreciation, in the long run it requires so little effort, but means so much to those you thank.

LESSON

Everyone, without exception, wants to feel that what they do for others is appreciated. If someone goes out of their way to do something nice for you, show them that it hasn't gone unnoticed by expressing your sincere gratitude. Although a simple "thank you" will always suffice, the more personal your expressions of gratitude are, the better, and the more likely you'll be to benefit from similar acts of kindness in the future.

IF IT WERE EASY,
EVERYONE WOULD DO IT

*"If it comes easy, if it doesn't require extraordinary effort,
you're not pushing hard enough: It's supposed to hurt like hell."*
—Dean Karnazes, *Ultramarathon Man*

Accomplishing meaningful personal goals requires hard work, sacrifice, and a willingness to persevere through pain and discomfort. It's never easy to do, nor should it be, given the rewards it provides. You could always make things easier on yourself by giving up once the going gets tough, but doing so won't help you grow, and sets a bad precedent for the next time you want to pursue something meaningful.

The more you opt for the easy way out because something is too hard, takes too long, or hurts too much, the more reliant you'll become on similar excuses in the future. It certainly doesn't help to be surrounded by advertising that promises you can have whatever you want (right now!), and that those instant gratifications can solve all of your problems. The not-so-subtle message is that things like love, happiness, and a small waistline are all just one purchase away, and require little, if any, effort on your part. The problem with taking these kinds of shortcuts, however, is that the results are never sustainable, and you forfeit any real chance to evolve as a person.

NO PAIN, NO GAIN

In order to grow and develop, you must experience some degree of pain and discomfort. Not surprisingly, most people will go to great lengths to avoid any *voluntary* pain or discomfort, and are reluctant to do anything the hard way (particularly when an abundance of easier options are available). But easier does not always mean better, and choosing comfort over challenge will not produce the same type of growth or happiness. Anyone who has voluntarily taken on adversity to complete a meaningful goal can attest to this. Whether your goal is to lose weight, improve your grades, or become a better person, stick to this simple rule of thumb: no pain (hard work and sacrifice), no gain (evolving and happiness).

Working hard to achieve a difficult goal doesn't mean being miserable 24/7, or that the rewards from your pursuit are wholly dependent upon the goal's completion. There is plenty of growth, satisfaction, and enjoyment to be had along the way, *if* you believe in the purpose of your mission. If you don't believe wholeheartedly in what you're trying to accomplish, you'll likely view any effort or sacrifice you have to make as a bother rather than as a necessary step in your development. That's why it helps to be selective and to deliberate *beforehand* whether the goal you're contemplating is worthy of your maximum effort.

Although going through this exercise in no way guarantees that your task will be easy, or that you'll achieve every goal you decide to take on, at least you'll be giving yourself the best chance to succeed. Accomplishing meaningful personal goals is hard enough; the last thing you need is to suffer unnecessarily because you're unsure whether your pursuit is even worth it.

One thing you can count on is that your path to success will be littered with obstacles, some of them seemingly insurmountable. The question is: how will you deal with them? I've noticed that the people who are most successful are those who never give up on their dreams because of setbacks or impediments. If anything, these hindrances motivate successful people to sharpen their focus and redouble their efforts in going after what they want.

A useful way to think about obstacles is that they are there for a reason: to weed out those who have anything less than a burning desire to go after what they want. Those who have only a moderate desire will take one glimpse at a difficult obstacle and begin to retreat or fold, while those with an unwavering resolve will do whatever is necessary to get to the other side of that obstruction by negotiating a plan around it, leaping over it, or bursting right through it.

> "Between you and every goal that you wish to achieve, there is a series of obstacles; and the bigger the goal, the bigger the obstacles. Your decision to be, have, and do something out of the ordinary entails facing difficulties and challenges that are out of the ordinary as well. Sometimes your greatest asset is simply your ability to stay with it longer than anyone else."
>
> —Brian Tracy

IT'S NOT SUPPOSED TO BE EASY

A number of years ago, I began training to run my first marathon. I was never a big runner, so I knew I had my work cut out for me, but it was a goal I'd always dreamed of pursuing and was committed to seeing through. Toward the end of my training, though, I found myself getting close to giving up the pursuit. The runs were just too long, and taking too much of a toll on me mentally and physically. Although the race was only a few months away, I started to think of excuses that would justify giving up on my goal prematurely: "I don't want a permanent injury." "I think I'm busy that weekend." "Only weirdos run marathons."

But just as I was ready to give up, a revelation dawned on me: *this isn't supposed to be easy.* Once I actually said those words to myself, it changed

IF IT WERE EASY, EVERYONE WOULD DO IT

the whole perception of what I was trying to do. If it were easy, everyone and their grandma would be running marathons every weekend, but they're not, and for good reason. It takes a significant amount of hard work and sacrifice for most people to train for and finish a marathon, and if I was going to do this, I would have to work through prolonged periods of pain and discomfort in order to accomplish my goal.

Once I fully understood and embraced this concept, I was able to push through the rest of my training and complete the marathon. Not only did I accomplish something I once considered beyond my reach, but by refusing to take an easy exit despite enormous discomfort, I also evolved as a person.

CONSEQUENCES CAN BE POWERFUL MOTIVATORS

If all else fails and you still find yourself struggling to stick to your original goal, there is another strategy you can implement to help you succeed: ensure that there will be real consequences if you give up on your pursuit prematurely. In particular, financial and/or social consequences.

Financial and social consequences are highly effective motivators when it comes to staying the course in pursuit of a meaningful goal. From a financial standpoint, spending money on nonrefundable items related to your goal (preferably in advance) will provide plenty of incentive to follow through on your plans. No one likes to part ways with their money without getting something in return, and doing this ensures that you'll at least think twice before calling it quits.

From a social standpoint, revealing what you plan to accomplish to those whose opinion you value will also make the idea of retreating seem far less attractive. It's one thing to slack off on your goal while no one else is looking, but when others have a genuine interest in your progress and are supporting you, you'll have strong incentive to give your best effort and see your goal through to the end.

Most of us are great at *setting* lofty goals, but run into problems following through on them once we realize how much work is involved. That's why this strategy is so effective. By deliberately arranging a system of consequences that discourages you from capitulating prematurely, you'll be giving yourself that needed nudge to get over any inevitable resistance and reach your goal.[7]

A JOURNEY OF A THOUSAND MILES STARTS WITH A SINGLE STEP

No matter what your goal is, getting started is usually the hardest part, so it's important to get through that first step without discouraging yourself with thoughts of the bigger picture. Running a marathon of twenty-six miles, or dropping a few inches from your waistline, can seem daunting if you only focus on the entirety of the task. Instead of letting yourself get bogged down before you even start, just focus on completing that first mile or losing that first pound. If you take things step by step, you'll soon discover that motion leads to momentum, and what once seemed like an impossible task, is now well within your grasp.

> "Success is the sum of small efforts, repeated day in and day out."
>
> —Robert Collier

Of course, you'll still have to work hard and overcome periods of pain and discomfort in order to reach your goal, but nothing worthwhile ever comes easy. If you want to experience the kind of growth and happiness that result from overcoming adversity, you have to find a way to persevere. By doing this, the next time you're faced with a similar challenge, you'll have the confidence to know that, although it won't be easy, you'll do whatever it takes to get through it, just as you did before.

---

7 Check out *www.stickk.com,* a great website that helps you utilize this very strategy to accomplish your goals.

--- LESSON ---

Accomplishing meaningful personal goals isn't supposed to be easy, whether it's losing weight, earning a promotion, or running a marathon. If these things were easy, everyone could achieve them with very little effort, and we wouldn't experience the same kind of growth and happiness that comes from reaching goals the hard way. By fully embracing this concept, you'll realize you're more than capable of achieving goals you once considered beyond your reach.

LIFE NATURALLY CYCLES

25

"When you get into a tight place and everything goes against you, till it seems as though you could not hold on a minute longer, never give up then, for that is just the place and time that the tide will turn."
—Harriet Beecher Stowe

Life is a long journey, full of many ups and downs. When facing some of life's most difficult challenges—the loss of a job, a broken heart, the death of a loved one—it's easy to believe that the sky is falling and that things will never get better. Although it's difficult to imagine a bright future in the midst of a down cycle, the good news is you won't feel that way forever. As life goes on and you gain more perspective, you'll realize that time is an amazing healer, and that you're more than capable of overcoming life's unexpected downturns. So no matter how gloomy your darkest days may seem at the time, always keep in mind that they won't last forever, and you *will* see better days.

NOTHING VERY BAD LASTS FOR VERY LONG

The cycles of life are as fascinating as they are inevitable. When we're deeply mired in a down cycle, we think that we're doomed forever, and when we're cruising high in an up cycle, we think that the good times will never end. But neither way of thinking is accurate, because not only are our external circumstances constantly changing, but so is our level of expectation.

Despite the fear that life will never be the same after an unforeseen setback, all of us have an uncanny ability to adapt to, and overcome, difficult life circumstances. The reason we're so resilient is that we tend to adjust our expectations based on how we feel right now, in the present. For example, when things are going well and we're feeling high on life, any small improvement in our circumstances won't seem very significant, since we're already *expecting* things to go well. But when we're feeling down in the dumps, and expecting things to stay that way, that same small improvement can seem like a major triumph.

The worse-off you feel, the greater the impact small improvements will have on your current well-being, and the easier they'll be to attain. This downward adjustment to expectations helps explain why things always seem their worst before they get better. By the time you reach the low point in a down cycle, you'll have adjusted your expectations to the point where almost any positive development in your life will feel like a considerable improvement. As time goes on, these improvements start to build momentum, and eventually help lift you out of your down cycle and into a new up cycle. So whenever you think things couldn't get any worse for you, just hang on a bit longer, because that's exactly when your life is about to turn around.

> "Cycles are self-correcting, and their reversal is not necessarily dependent on [external] events. They reverse (rather than going on forever) because trends create the reasons for their own reversal. Thus, I like to say success carries within itself the seeds of failure, and failure the seeds of success."
>
> —Howard Marks, *The Most Important Thing*

THIS, TOO, SHALL PASS

I didn't enjoy high school very much. By the time I was a senior, I had lost all of my friends, got picked on regularly, and couldn't get a date if my life depended on it (did I mention my GPA had also fallen off a cliff?). I was miserable on a daily basis and couldn't picture a scenario where things would ever get better. There were times during that period where I asked myself if life was really worth living, and even contemplated suicide.

I don't know if I could have ever gone through with killing myself, but I was in the midst of a serious down cycle, and wasn't wise enough to realize that, as bad as it was, this too would pass (and it did). Now when I look back on that dark period in my life, I can't believe I let myself get so discouraged. All of the things I was so depressed over seem so trivial to me in retrospect, because I've lived long enough to put them in their proper perspective.

I've gone on to experience many other down cycles since then due to failed relationships, job losses, and the death of my mom. As difficult as those setbacks were to deal with at the time, none of them lasted forever, and I did live to see happier days.

That's the crucial point to always keep in mind. When you're growing up, you have to trust that, no matter how devastating something might seem at any given moment, it won't seem as life-shattering when you're older and have a broader perspective. No one is saying you shouldn't feel sad or grief when something unpleasant occurs in your life, but it's important to remind yourself that those feelings will abate over time, and that your life will cycle up again.

YOU ARE NOT ALONE

Picturing a bright future when you're busy feeling depressed is never easy, particularly when you have limited life experience to fall back on. Fortunately, no matter what issue you're struggling with, there are countless people who have successfully navigated a similar path to the one you're on now, and you should utilize every resource available to tap into their wisdom. Whether that wisdom comes from a parent, teacher, mentor, or even a book, learning from those who have been there before you can help put your problems in their proper perspective, and provide the much-needed comfort of knowing that, as bad as things seem now, life does go on, and you will see better days.

LESSON

Life naturally cycles up and down all the time. As interminable as your darkest days may seem during any given down cycle, they won't last forever, and your life will cycle up again. Most people learn this as they grow older and accumulate life experience. But in the absence of that, it helps to rely on the guidance of those who have already been in your shoes, lived through similar life cycles, and possess a broader perspective.

OTHER ESSENTIAL LESSONS

Below are several life lessons that are more pragmatic than the twenty-five already discussed, but no less essential.

INSURE YOURSELF

At a minimum, I believe everyone should be covered by the following insurance:

- Medical/Dental
- Life (if you have a spouse and/or children)
- Homeowners/Renters
- Disability (if you work)
- Auto

We all have a tendency to think that nothing bad will ever happen to us. ("I'll never get in an accident." "No one is going to rob my house." "I'll never get sick.") However, the unexpected can and does happen—to *all* of us. I completely understand that insurance can be costly (especially medical), but the tradeoff of peace of mind you receive is well worth the investment. I'm not saying to go out and buy every type of insurance out there, but at a minimum take care of the basics.[8]

The first thing I would always do whenever I was between jobs was to buy short-term medical insurance. It pained me to do so because I had to spend money when I wasn't employed, but I knew that not doing this would make me vulnerable to a *catastrophic loss*. And that's the main value that insurance provides: prevention of total financial ruin.

Whether it's extensive flood damage from a freak storm, or sky-high medical bills from an unexpected illness or injury, the last thing you want is to get wiped out financially in one shot. Not only that, but leaving

---

8 Check with your employer and credit card companies first to understand what types of insurance coverage they may already be providing for you.

yourself vulnerable to extreme loss may indirectly put your loved ones in a precarious position if they ever had to support you. So please give yourself peace of mind, and get insured in the basics.

When my mom had a relapse of cancer soon after retiring from her job, she had to undergo extensive chemotherapy treatments that totaled in the hundreds of thousands of dollars. Thankfully, she had had the foresight to purchase extensive medical coverage for her post-retirement years that covered most of her treatments. Having proper medical insurance helped alleviate a major worry for my mom, and when you're dealing with health problems, the loss of a job, or an unexpected disaster, one less worry is always a good thing. Remember, you can't predict, but you can prepare.

KEEP A JOURNAL

There's no better way to track the progress of your life than by keeping a journal. A journal can be used to record anything from memorable experiences to useful life lessons, and often provides entertaining reading as you get older. ("Did I really do that, think that, or act like that?")

I started writing in a journal when I was in my mid-twenties, and one of my biggest regrets is that I didn't start sooner. It would have been so fascinating to read about what my mindset was like when I was starting puberty, struggling through high school, or discovering myself in college. However, I'm just glad that I have a journal at all, because I now have a useful reference to analyze my personal development throughout life.

A journal doesn't have to mean a daily log of routine activities, such as what meals you ate or how long you slept, and it certainly shouldn't feel like an obligation. Instead, you should use it to record anything that has significance for your life, such as a memorable experience, an important lesson, a useful idea, a goal you'd like to achieve, or an improvement you'd like to make. In fact, it can really be anything that you want to remember, refer back to, or remind yourself of.

Once you start a journal, it's just as important to maintain it. A good way to do this is to set aside a few minutes at the end of each day, week, or month for both reflection and writing. Another method I've found helpful is to write down anything journal-worthy as soon as it pops into your head. Even if it's just jotting down a few quick words to contemplate at a later time, at least it will help you avoid losing the thought altogether. In the past I would often forget important ideas and revelations by waiting too long to record them on paper, and now I know better than to rely on just memory alone.

Remember, just because you're late doesn't mean you shouldn't start. A journal is useful at any age, and all you need to get started is a notebook, a pen, and your thoughts.

SAVE EARLY AND OFTEN

Someone once said money grows on the tree of patience, but that sage advice appears to have been long forgotten. In today's reality, any disposable income left over after paying the rent, feeding the family, and gassing up the car usually gets exhausted on other financial "priorities" such as the latest high-tech gadgets, new designer outfits, and various other short-lived enjoyments. This is too bad, because although it sounds less sexy, saving early and often provides *far* greater benefits over the long run than splurging on material goods ever will.

For starters, savings can be held and accumulated in an interest-bearing account, like a money market or CD.[9] As soon as you put your money into one of these savings vehicles, compound interest begins to grow your balance exponentially, as if by magic. I've seen enough charts to know that saving early, and consistently, allows compound interest to boost your savings in a major way, so the earlier you start the better. The best part is you don't even have to lift a finger to generate all of that additional *free* money; compound interest does all the work for you!

Another benefit of saving early and often is that it helps provide you with sufficient financial reserves in case something unexpected ever happens,

---

9   As I write this in May 2012, money market and CD rates pay close to 0% interest, and have been that way for a number of years. However, the current ultra-low savings rate won't last forever, and shouldn't deter you from getting in the habit of saving early and often.

like the loss of a job. If this recent financial crisis has taught us anything, it's that having sufficient savings can mean the difference between staying afloat through the storm, and potential financial ruin.

But being financially prepared for the unexpected isn't just about avoiding potential crises. It's also about having the wherewithal to take advantage of life's unforeseen *opportunities,* such as starting your own business, furthering your education, or pursuing a lifelong dream.

Finally, saving early and often increases your financial security, which leads to greater freedom. It's much easier to choose the passion you want to pursue, the place you want to live, and the way you spend your time, when money isn't an impediment to those decisions.

Putting money toward savings may seem like slow progress, but if you start early and stick with it, the benefits only get better over time. Once you commit to regularly saving, compound interest will work its magic on growing your balance, your freedom to choose will continue to expand, and you'll be well-positioned to handle life's unexpected challenges and opportunities.

PREPARE FOR THE UNEXPECTED

Death can be a scary topic to contemplate, and it's understandable why many people are reluctant to discuss what they'd want done if they ever died unexpectedly, or were near death and unable to communicate. It's much easier to believe that nothing like that could ever happen and avoid the topic entirely. But there's real value in having these difficult, candid discussions. Telling someone you love and trust about how you'd want things handled in the unfortunate event that you're unable to decide for yourself, spares the people you care about additional heartache by having to collectively guess at what you *may have* wanted.

With that in mind, one of the first things I did when I got married was to go over these exact kinds of scenarios with my wife, just in case. Believe me, there are much more uplifting topics I would have rather been discussing with her, such as where we should go on our next vacation, or what we should name our kids. However, despite my sometimes youthful arrogance,

I know that the unexpected *can* happen, and in case it does, I don't want my family to agonize unnecessarily over what I may have wanted.

If you don't feel comfortable talking about such delicate topics openly, at least put your wishes down somewhere in writing (like in a journal), and let someone know where they can find it if need be. Doing this will help eliminate any potential ambiguities and second-guessing of your intentions. Here is what I wrote in my own journal:

> If I'm ever in a coma, on a respirator, or in a vegetative state: If the prospects of me recovering or returning to living a normal life aren't realistic, then I don't want to be kept alive.

> If I die: I would like all of my organs donated. I also want to be cremated (no open wake, they'll never get my hair right!) and would prefer a spiritual memorial service limited to friends and family. All of my money and possessions should go to my wife.

Discussing or even thinking about these kinds of things is never easy. But by taking the time to prepare for the unexpected, at least you'll have the peace of mind that your wishes will be carried out as you desire, and that your loved ones won't suffer unnecessarily trying to determine what's best for you.

AFTERWORD

If you asked me what the goal of life is, I'd say it's to be as happy as possible, and to avoid any unnecessary suffering. I'd also add that the best way to achieve those ends is to seek out, and adhere to, life's timeless lessons, such as those included in this book.

The context of our lives will change over time due to cultural shifts, new technology, and various other factors, but the essential lessons of life itself are everlasting. As humans we all share the same predictable fears, insecurities, hopes, and desires, just by simply existing. We're all in this together, and as a consequence of our shared humanity, we should continue to search for the timeless lessons that help us all find our way to happy and live better lives.

> "Yes, the world is changing, and will continue to do so. But that does not mean we should stop the search for timeless principles. Think of it this way: While the practices of engineering continually evolve and change, the laws of physics remain relatively fixed. I like to think of our work as a search for timeless principles ... that will remain true and relevant no matter how the world changes around us. Yes, the specific application will change (the engineering), but certain immutable laws of organized human performance (the physics) will endure."
> —Jim Collins, *Good to Great*

When aspiring to live a meaningful and happy life, we make the best decisions we can with the knowledge we have at the time. I sincerely hope this book serves as a useful guide for you when making those decisions, and I wish you the best on your life's journey.

SUGGESTED READING

The books listed below have improved my life immeasurably. I hope they do the same for you.

ATLAS SHRUGGED
(AYN RAND)

An epic novel that encourages you to go after what you deserve in this life, without feeling the need to apologize for it.

THE DEATH OF IVAN ILYICH
(LEO TOLSTOY)

If you only read one of the books on this list, make sure it's this. This book ignited my passion for reading and learning about life, and I reread it every year. It reminds you of how short life is, and makes you question whether you're living your life the right way.

THE PARADOX OF CHOICE
(BARRY SCHWARTZ)

An eye-opening book that squashes the assumption that more is always better. Reading the chapter on adaptation is a must.

THE POWER OF NOW
(ECKHART TOLLE)

No better book on explaining what it means to live in the present, and the futility of holding onto worries outside of your control.

THE STORY OF MY EXPERIMENTS WITH TRUTH
(MOHANDAS K. GANDHI)

This book literally changed my life. Gandhi's autobiography is a pure reflection of what it means to live your life according to truth, and will make you view the world around you in a whole new light.

STUMBLING ON HAPPINESS
(DANIEL GILBERT)

A brilliant book that explains why we are terrible predictors of the future, and equally bad at presuming what will make us happy.

TOO SOON OLD, TOO LATE SMART
(GORDON LIVINGSTON)

Gordon Livingston has all of the requisite experience and knowledge to be considered an authority on life. His book of essential truths should be required reading for adolescents and adults alike.

ACKNOWLEDGEMENTS

There's no such thing as a self-made man. I have many people to thank for the person I am today, not to mention the writing of this book.

I'd first like to thank David Driscoll, Lawrence Dunning, and Joe Sovcik for their help in critiquing the earliest drafts. I wasn't much of a writer back then and know how torturous that must have been!

I'd also like to thank my brother, Chris, and sister-in-law, Deya, for all their insightful suggestions and creative input, as well as my wife, Ginetta, for tolerating my nightly retreats to the bedroom to write.

I'd especially like to thank my mom. So many of these lessons I learned because of her, and without her this book would not have been possible.

Finally, I'd like to thank you, the reader. The goal of this book is to help people find their way to happy and live better lives, and I'm grateful to you for reading it.

Contact Brad Anastasia at:
reservehouse@gmail.com

Or visit:
www.bradanastasia.com

ABOUT THE AUTHOR

BRAD ANASTASIA has a keen understanding of what it takes to live a good life, despite having learned that practical wisdom the hard way.

After struggling with depression, poor grades, and a criminal record during his teenage years, he implemented a number of long-overdue changes in his life and went on to become a standout student athlete at the University of Chicago.

Upon graduating with a degree in psychology, he secured a lucrative investment banking position in New York City. But despite promotions and a six-figure salary, he discovered that the traditional path to material success wasn't what it's cracked up to be, and gave it all up to travel through South America in pursuit of a simpler life.

The lessons learned as a result of these and countless other experiences helped him gain an intuitive understanding of how to live a happy and meaningful life. His mission now is to share that hard-earned wisdom with others so they can avoid the same unnecessary struggles, make smarter life choices, and improve their well-being.

Born and raised on Long Island, New York, Brad has lived and worked in a number of different cities throughout the world, including Lima, Peru and Buenos Aires, Argentina. He currently resides in Chicago with his wife, Ginetta.

16134002R00087

Made in the USA
Lexington, KY
07 July 2012